# VICIOUS CIRCLES MANUAL

## ANGER MANAGEMENT FOR MEN

# Stephen C. Simmer, LICSW, PhD

Reach Educational Seminars

VICIOUS CIRCLES MANUAL: ANGER MANAGEMENT FOR
MEN

# TABLE OF CONTENTS

# INTRODUCTION

## Becoming Firemen

This is a manual for men. The manual is an attempt to recruit volunteer firemen—volunteers not to hose down buildings, but to save our lives and the lives of those we love from the fire of our

own anger. Left unchecked, this inner fire erupts in violence against loved ones, destroys our families, loses our jobs, and alienates us from our children, from intimate partners, and from ourselves. Domestic violence occurs in a third of marriages. Inappropriate anger in the workplace is the primary cause of job loss. Road rage kills thousands and injures tens of thousands of people annually. There is growing evidence that an angry, hostile attitude is more dangerous to the heart than is cigarette smoking, high cholesterol, or high blood pressure (Goleman, p. 170). Every week, there are high-profile stories in the newspaper of murders, violence in sports, and arrests of athletes or movie stars for domestic violence.

Firemen do more than simply extinguish blazes, of course. They inspect buildings for potential fire hazards, enforce standards of fire prevention such as sprinkler systems, placement of extinguishers, or smoke alarms, help develop emergency evacuation protocols, and investigate after a fire to determine cause. I recently spoke to a fireman of 30 years, and he told me how dramatically his job had changed since the development of smoke alarms. Before, fires would often be undiscovered until the building was enveloped in flames, so there were frequent conflagrations which would involve the work of departments from several towns. Often their main job was to stop the fire from spreading to adjacent buildings, because the first building was lost. With the development of smoke alarms, the fire department is usually contacted much sooner. With a few exceptions, the fire can be put out easily, and now the firemen can spend more time playing cards and shining the engines.

The job of anger management is similar. An essential part of the job is extinguishing angry blazes, of course. But if we can develop a system of anger sensors which detect anger when it is small, if we can develop the "evacuation protocol" of time-out, if we can place extinguishing thoughts at "places" where anger is likely to break out, our jobs will be made significantly easier.

## A Note to Men

Many of the ideas and techniques in this book would apply to anyone with anger problems. But men have particular problems with anger—not so much in the frequency of their anger (some studies have shown that women experience anger more often), but in the emotional and physical destructiveness of the anger. Men cause ninety-five percent of injuries from domestic violence. Why has this happened?

Some have suggested that it is permissible in our society for men to be angry, but forbidden that they be sad, while it is the reverse for women. This is at least partially true. Movies, the military, sports, and music tell men that *anger is the defining moment in a man's life.* It is remarkable how frequently a moment of justified anger is the climax of film, play, or novel. The story development often hinges on the gradual build of anger in the hero. Insults are endured, the slings and arrows of outrageous fortune are suffered. The bad guy sneers and spits, kicks dirt, shoots the preacher, steps on the hero's hat, and steals the girl's farm. The patient endurance of the reluctant hero finally gives way to action. Hamlet picks up his sword, Shane straps on his gun, Achilles dons his armor and prepares to battle Hector. The story shifts into high gear with this decision by the hero that enough is enough, it's the last straw, they've gone too far. Patient endurance gives way to angry action. This shift is often seen as the crucial rite of passage of achieving manhood. Football coaches and military leaders exploit this idea, challenging the young men in their care to demonstrate their manhood by becoming angry at the villains who so fully deserve what's coming to them.

Men are told, "Get mad!" But at the same time, society gives an equally strong message that anger is wrong. Anger is the leading cause of job firings. It leads to expulsion from games or even from the sport altogether. Inappropriate anger in the home gets men arrested for domestic violence, and results in children being removed by social services. Marriage manuals decry not only physical violence, but also verbal abuse that comes with anger. Child-rearing manuals point out that corporal punishment and anger directed at children makes it more likely that they will become violent, antisocial adults with poor self-esteem and even a lower income.

Men receive contradictory messages from our culture: in one ear they hear "Get angry!" and in the other ear they hear "Don't get angry!" As a result, they become extremely confused about how to handle this powerful emotion. They become strange hybrid creatures, like the centaur or sphinx of Greek mythology, with two opposing strategies of anger management. They try to fulfill the contradictory demands in a number of ways: They may alternate between cool boredom and rage, blow up cities while sitting dispassionately at a computer screen, deny any feeling at all while they are in the middle of a loud argument.

What can we do? In obeying the contradictory demands, we have a primitive strategy of anger management: I stuff my anger

down my own throat, or stuff it down someone else's throat. This is like playing golf with only two golf clubs, like trying to compose music with only two notes of the scale. We need more options at our disposal in working with anger, and this is one goal of this manual.

> *Cultural Influences Assignment: On worksheet 2 at the back of the manual, write down a favorite cartoon character from childhood, three movies which have taught you something about men and anger, and three songs that have messages about anger. Sum up what you have learned from each.*

## But I Almost Never Get Mad…

Often a person tells me, "But I almost never get mad. I don't have an anger problem. It only happens once in a blue moon."

I don't know if there was a blue moon the night of April 14, 1912, when the Titanic hit the iceberg. I don't know if there was one, or two, or a thousand icebergs in the north Atlantic that night. I do know that the newspapers called the ship "unsinkable," and that the owners were so certain of this they reduced the number of lifeboats to save space on deck and sailed at top speed to save time. And I know that the Titanic hit only *one* iceberg—not two, not a thousand.

*Did the Titanic have an iceberg problem?* Of course—no matter how many icebergs there were. And the problem wasn't the iceberg; it was the blithe self-confidence that led to ignoring icebergs. Suppose a man only gets really angry once, then murders his ex-wife and her boyfriend. If this is not an anger problem, it is certainly a major legal problem, despite the fact that "it was only an isolated incident."

Furthermore, with the Titanic it was not the iceberg that could be seen that was the problem—that may have been only a small tip protruding from the water. It was the huge mass of the nine-tenths below the surface that did the damage to the hull. A violent incident may be rare, but is generally the visible tip of patterns of thinking and behaving that are far more extensive, and perhaps just as damaging. Preceding every violent incident is a vast pyramid of preparatory thought and action from childhood to the present, and if these patterns could have been arrested earlier, the violent act might never have emerged.

If we were in charge of averting iceberg problems, we would probably arrange a diligent iceberg watch, maybe involving round-

the-clock shifts of observers perched on the ship's bow, or high-tech sonar or radar sensors that could detect icebergs significantly in advance. To avoid anger problems, we need something similar—a sophisticated anger-watch, detecting anger from a distance, along with an emergency escape plan if something unexpected happens. We need to avoid at all costs the delusion that we are "unsinkable," because this sets the stage for calamity.

# The Adventures of Ben and Bill and their **Bears**

Ben and Bill each have a bear.

Bill says something, and arouses Ben's bear.

Ben's bear grows larger. Ben grows smaller. Ben's bear fires something back, awakening Bill's bear. The bears are unchained.

Both Ben's bear and Bill's bear are very large and strong. Both Ben and Bill are small and weak. Nothing much that they do has any effect on the bears.

No more Ben and Bill.

# I.   VICIOUS CIRCLES

I remember in childhood being trapped on a Ferris wheel for what seemed like hours.  The operator had left for an unexplained break, and the ride changed from an adventure to a queasy, monotonous nightmare.  At key times in our lives, we each have glimpsed our lives

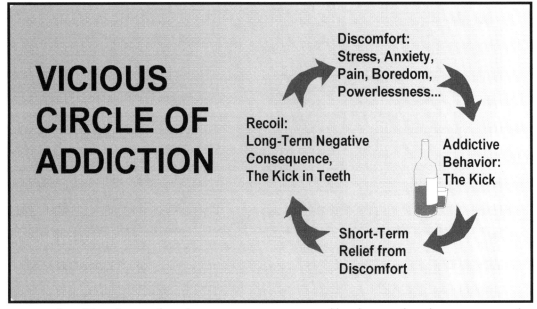

as stuck Ferris wheels—rat races, tailspins, broken records, whirlpools.  According to Sigmund Freud, one of the key characteristics of neurosis is the compulsion to repeat—needing to do something over and over.  This remains one of the key characteristics of psychological problems—endless repetition that is both senseless and destructive.  This repetition is found in problems with anxiety, depression, and in various addictions: we are caught in a tailspin we can't stop.

# Addiction as Vicious Circles

What is addiction? Many definitions are possible. It is a habit, but obviously more than that. Brushing one's teeth is a habit, but we don't call it an addiction. Breathing or walking upright are habits, too, but not addictions. An addiction is some pattern of behavior that seems necessary, but in the end it is not. It also must be destructive in an unexpected way.

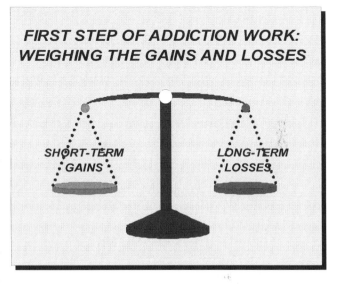

*An addiction is a vicious circle of behavior driven by a short-term kick and a long-term kick in the teeth.* A person is in a condition of discomfort, and a certain behavior promises an end to that discomfort. This is the "kick." However, if the same behavior is repeated, the discomfort increases in the long run—the "kick in the teeth." For example, a man might feel stressed by a hard day's work, and might decide to stop off at a bar for some stress reduction. After one drink, the stress seems to lift some, so he repeats this behavior several times to make sure the stress is done and gone for good. Stress managed at last, he may get into his car to drive home, only to be stopped by a state trooper, who increases his stress by arresting him for DWI. After spending the night in jail, he returns home to his wife, who is quite upset at the fact that he was drunk the night before, and she criticizes him eloquently for his irresponsibility. Stress increases again. If this man decides to reduce stress again in the customary way of drinking, the vicious circle is complete, and he is showing signs of addiction.

Obviously, there are addictions aside from those involving chemicals. One may be addicted to chocolate, gambling, sex, risk, spending, the internet. In each case, there is an immediate reward followed by an eventual punishment, which sets one in search of the reward again. The first step of addiction work is weighing the short-term gains against the long-term losses: am I getting what I want? It is not often recognized that anger, too, may be an addiction. But an addiction to what? What is the immediate reward that lures one into the vicious circle? *The reward that drives anger addiction is the feeling of power that generally results from angry words and actions.* Short-term, one may get what he desires. He is the 2000-pound gorilla who sits anywhere he wants, King Kong who receives the offerings of the local tribes. A person may feel he receives respect, love, obedience, attention, or his favorite TV channel if he gets angry. But what are the long-term consequences of anger?

---

*Assignment: On Worksheet 4, reflect on your anger for a moment, and write down the assets or advantages of anger in the left column, and the liabilities or disadvantages of anger in the right column. For example, one might feel he gains from his anger because it makes him clearer about his needs, but might find he loses from it because it gets him into trouble at work.*

*When you are finished with the worksheet, look it over. Were there more positives or negatives? Return to this exercise as you proceed through this workbook to see if new advantages or disadvantages occur to you. It is useful to ask yourself this sort of question after every incident of anger or irritation: did I get what I wanted? Was my anger my friend or enemy in that situation?*

---

## The Tree of Anger Addiction

There are several typical Vicious Circles of power addiction, which are similar to branches on a tree. Like branches, they are distinct from one another, yet at the same time different aspects of the same tree, joining together at the trunk.

Each of the six is driven by a value that is admirable in its own right—love, justice, order, respect, peace, and freedom. One could call these six forms of power in a positive sense, because feeling empowered is a worthy goal. However, each form of positive power gets subverted in the self-destructive whirlpool of the Vicious Circle, and the opposite of the original value is created. Dr. Frankenstein tried to create the ideal human, but instead created a monster, and this is true of each of the six Vicious Circles of anger.

The Tree of Anger Addiction

## Vicious Circle: Rage for Order

When this vicious circle is dominant, a person becomes anxious when things are out of order, chaotic, or in disarray. He has a strong sense for the way things should be, and is often anxious or irritated with things as they are. Things in life don't move smoothly. Often anger is used as a weapon to rectify imbalances, to set things right. This person is a doer, and it is particularly difficult for him to simply

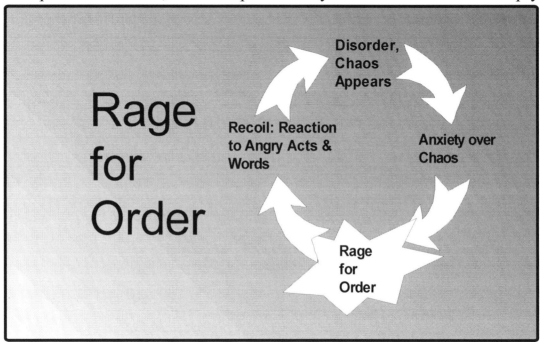

let things ride, to accept things that can't be changed, to go with the rise and fall of events. The ironic result of the addiction to control is that anger contributes to the chaos--things get worse, not better.

Like the other Vicious Circles, there is a goal in Rage for Order which is a noble value. The search for an orderly world, for an orderly life is quite positive, and this urge underlies science, philosophy, and the forces of civilization—every human endeavor which has sought to make the world more rational and systematic. However, anger ironically turns this quest for order into an urge for disruption and discord. For examples of this vicious circle, one need not look just to the extremes—Adolf Hitler with his dream of order and purity, which ironically created anarchy and upheaval throughout the world, and the atrocity of the death camps. We can find examples much closer to home. A man has a stepdaughter who is using marijuana. He criticizes her drug use, and she shouts profanities at him. Furious, in the name of discipline and authority over the household, he hits her. His wife calls the police, and he is arrested for assault. Furious with his wife for this betrayal, he files for divorce. Chaos reigns.

## Vicious Circle: Mad about You

A person caught in this vicious circle often feels anxious over the prospect of being abandoned by a partner. One tends to oscillate between dependency and a dramatized independence, but there is frequently a sense of emptiness or panic when he is alone for any extended period. This person is apt to be a relationship addict, and like any addict goes drunk and dry, but moderation is difficult. He desires another to know him very well, so well his partner is able to read his mind, to know his needs before he knows them himself. This may cause him to try to control his partner in an effort to stave off the abandonment he fears. Relationships tend to be intense and stormy, and this is alternately gratifying and frustrating.

The most intolerable situation imaginable for this type of person is sexual betrayal—discovering his wife or girlfriend cheating on him with someone else. He believes powerfully that he *owns* his intimate partner—*his* wife, *his* girlfriend. Slavery ended in this country well over a century ago, but in spite of this, he believes he has property rights, which entitle him to do whatever he wishes to what belongs to him. This sense of sexual ownership may continue long after separation and divorce. He may continue to stalk, ruminate about her betrayal, call on the telephone, violate restraining orders, or war with her over the children.

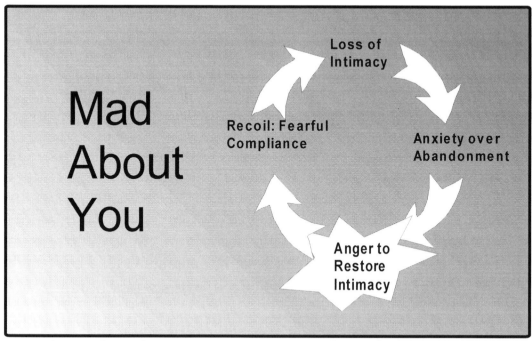

Anger here is an attempt to create love, but instead it creates hurt, mistrust, hatred and fear. The man's wife may placate her angry or violent partner, but it is rare that anyone would wish intimacy with a person who is threatening, dangerous, and explosive. The angry person's partner keeps secrets out of fear, and this creates yet more distance and alienation in the relationship, causing the circle to turn again.

## Vicious Circle: The Shame-Game

The trigger for anger in this situation is shame--shame over appearing foolish, over not being strong enough, mature enough, big enough--enough in general. Shame is a feeling of *public* powerlessness—the brand of cowardice, the pilgrim in the stocks with the sign around his neck. This person's biggest nightmare is the

ANGER
TO REMEDY
SHAME

jeering crowd, the patronizing pat on the head. Shame leads to anger, and anger is a drive to overcome the shame, to be big enough, strong enough, man enough. Anger places one momentarily in the dominant role as The Strong One, but this is not enough, because anger violates others either in violent acts or hurtful words.

Recoil may come from outside—additional public humiliation—or from within. In internal recoil, anger provokes guilt, and guilt causes a person to crawl back and beg forgiveness. "I can't believe what I did, what I said. Please forgive me—I'll never do that again." But the submissive role leads again to shame, and the circle continues to spin. An example of this vicious circle is found in Tennessee Williams' *A Streetcar Named Desire*. Stanley Kowalski, playing cards with friends, tells his wife Stella and her sister Blanche to turn down the music. He loses a hand of poker, then jumps in annoyance from his chair and smashes the radio. When Stella criticizes him, he hits her. She flees with Blanche and goes upstairs to the neighbor's apartment. It is then that Stanley, racked with guilt, screams out his classic "Stella!" from the street. Stella slowly descends the stairs, and Stanley weeps, hugging her in the submissive position. But two scenes later in the play, Stanley has forgotten his submission, and is again angrily abusive.

Let's look at the other type of shame-game, where the recoil happens not because of an internal process of recognizing one's offenses, but from outside. Anger itself becomes shameful, and one is humiliated publicly—arrested, disciplined, one's reputation smeared. Shame is feeling smaller, inadequate in comparison with others.

Anger is often an attempt to restore power and status in an immediate way. For example, a man from a small town gets into an argument with his wife in their home over her failure to back him up in disciplining his stepson. He is trying to remedy is inferior condition

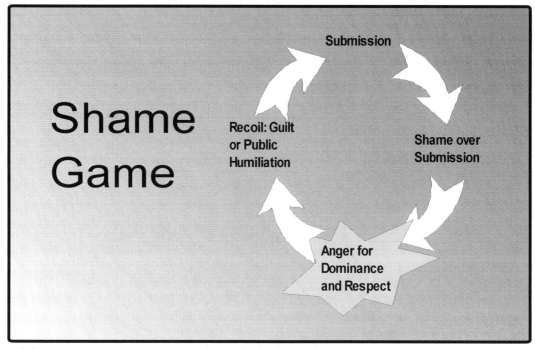

with anger. He gets so agitated during the argument that she threatens to call the police. Terrified of the potential humiliation in front of the townspeople who know him well, he wrestles with her for the phone. He lets go suddenly, and the telephone hits her in the face. The police arrive and arrest the man for a domestic offense. The shame of going to court and attending an anger management group is almost unbearable. Here his feeling humiliated caused the original argument, and his anger was an attempt to rectify that. But this has led to an even more intense shame.

## Vicious Circle: Breaking Out

This person tends to react most strongly when things get in the way, close him in, when rules seem too restrictive. He uses anger to break out, to challenge authority, to burst through whatever obstacles stand between him and his freedom. The person feels that life should be a dance, but too often it is weighed down with unnecessary responsibilities and silly regulations. He wants to be the absolute master of his destiny, and when people or things stand in his way, he

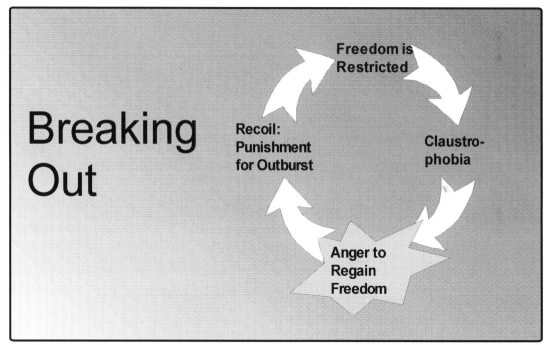

challenges them. His mottoes are "No one tells me what to do," and "Question authority." He is concerned that relationships might fence him in or tie him down. The primary trigger to anger is a feeling of claustrophobia.

Life recoils against this sort of anger, as well. The result is often not more freedom, but greater restriction. For example, a young man is caught by the hall monitor without a pass, and he threatens her angrily in an attempt to eliminate this seemingly ridiculous hindrance. The monitor reports the threat, and the young man faces suspension from school and charges of assault. What began as an attempt to regain freedom has produced greater blockage.

I worked once with a sixty-year-old man who was experiencing fury over the junior high school children in his neighborhood who strolled in front of his car in the mornings, impeding his progress as he tried to drive to work. Many years before, he had left his wife of twenty-five years, had quit his job as a political consultant, and had taken a position as a cowboy earning a few dollars a day, all in the name of freedom. His anger was mainly triggered by impediments—things or circumstances which frustrated his attempts to reach any goal, anything that restricted his freedom or corralled his spirit.

## Vicious Circle: Just Deserts

The person caught in the Just Deserts Vicious Circle sees the world as one that should be just and fair. If something happens which he sees as unfair, he experiences anger towards the person who has gotten better treatment, and also towards those who are responsible for dispensing justice. When he gets angry, it is in the interest of restoring the balance to the universe. With this person, the roots of this anger-trigger are often found in a relationship with a sibling during childhood. He often tells a brooding tale of a brother or sister who got easier treatment or special advantages. There may also be a story told of racial or ethnic injustice, perpetuated by an insensitive or malevolent social and judicial system that has stacked the deck in favor of others. When I asked Greg what sorts of feelings of discomfort triggered anger, he answered without hesitation, "Unfairness." This seemed an apt answer, at least at the start. But unfairness alone doesn't trigger anger. I have never spoken with anyone who got furious when he got the *biggest* piece of cake, although that situation would be as unfair objectively as when he gets

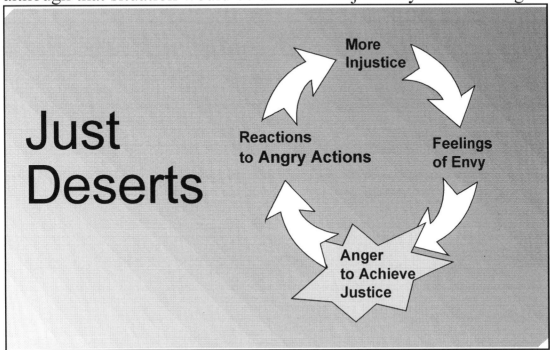

the smallest piece. The feeling at the core of unfairness is *envy*. The feeling of injustice is not a simple feeling of envy, which would be accompanied by the thought "I wish I could have a car like his." The thoughts that accompany the feeling of injustice are these:

1. **Life should be fair.** This is a thought that demands a just universe, where individuals are rewarded according to their relative merit: "I deserve a car like his as much as he does." "I work as hard as he does. I should have a house as nice as his."

2. **The powers that be blew the call.** This is the assumption of a power—human or spiritual—which has the job of keeping the universe in harmony according to the law mentioned above. This may be a person (boss, parent, referee, political figure), spiritual power (gods, angels), or a political system that is

responsible for maintaining the just universe. "Those jerks in the government have set it up so he gets a Porsche and I don't." "So why is it that the boss overlooks every good idea I have, and he can do no wrong?"

3. **I am the avenging angel, restoring justice.** This is a thought that assumes that I have the right to avenge injustice, to return the world to the harmony that has been lost. "The ref didn't see him giving me a cheap shot, so I'll get even by myself." "The little rat stepped on my foot, so I'll stomp on his."

One objection that may be raised here is this: "Wait, what if these stories are true? What if a person *has* been mistreated at work? What if an individual *is* a member of an oppressed minority? Isn't the anger justified, even necessary, as a way of balancing the scales?" In the descriptions of the Vicious Circles, I have not dealt with the issue of whether there is some truth to the belief system. For instance, in the Mad About You Vicious Circle, one might ask, "What if a man's wife is really having an affair. Isn't the anger justified then?" In response to this, I suggest that if we turn our longing for justice over to anger, it frequently backfires. In the process of avenging a wrong, the angry person often puts the universe even more out of harmony by doing something even more unjust. The social world reacts again, causing him even more problems because once again he sees himself as misunderstood, getting unfair treatment. To achieve true justice, we need a more sophisticated and thoughtful strategy than simply blowing up. This merely perpetuates the problem.

# Vicious Circle: Avoiding Anger

In the Avoiding Anger vicious circle, an individual has learned either from direct experience of anger—his own anger, another's anger, or both—that this is hazardous material, to be sidestepped at all costs. This person attempts to stay cool and calm. Feelings of all kinds are avoided, in fact, because they lead inevitably to upset. But escape is futile. A person tries to avoid anger, but it finds him anyway, just as ghosts in folktales can't be left behind forever. The coolness alternates with explosive heat. Avoiding anger ironically becomes another way of producing anger, anger of a particularly virulent kind. The person has two notes on the scale: cool boredom and rage, and the rage, even if rare, is disturbingly beyond control. One often has the sense that the other party has pressed the issue and

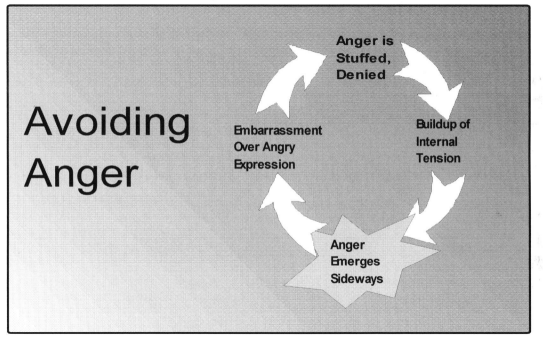

Avoiding Anger

Anger is Stuffed, Denied

Buildup of Internal Tension

Anger Emerges Sideways

Embarrassment Over Angry Expression

not allowed him to withdraw, as he would have preferred.

In this vicious circle, when small things happen with another person, the individual generally says little. He does not wish to cause a major stink, tells himself "it's no big deal." He then makes a small deposit into the *anger bank*, where it draws interest and grows. Finally, something small happens in the relationship that tips the balance, and the anger explodes with a vengeance.

When the anger does emerge, it is particularly indigestible by the party on the receiving end. First, it often emerges over a relatively small thing, causing the other bewilderment over the lack of proportion. "Why is he making such a big deal over the toothpaste cap?" Second, the angry person often brings out old things that have been festering in the anger bank for a while, causing the person on the receiving end to wonder, "Wow, why didn't he mention the fact he didn't like my sister when she was visiting last year?" Third, when the explosion does come, there are often so many things brought up at once, it is difficult to respond or make changes: "Well, there's no use. Everything I do is wrong." Because the anger is so big, indigestible, and irrelevant, the angry person re-learns the lesson that it does no good to let the anger surface, and the "stuffing" process begins anew.

There is a sub-species of this vicious circle, where the anger does not emerge in a "hot" way, but instead emerges in a cold, aloof way. The furious party says nothing, but simply withdraws further. If asked by the other party if there is something wrong, he responds that "Everything is just fine," but the non-verbal signals contradict this. The person on the receiving end has difficulty understanding what might be causing the icy fury, and again cannot digest the partner's anger.

The presence of this vicious circle seems confusing. Isn't the point of anger management to avoid potentially explosive situations? Why would this be a problem? There is often some confusion between anger *avoidance* and anger *management*. Avoiding anger only closets it, stores it for a later decision. It is like avoiding opening up bills. Eventually the table is stacked with bills, and the collection agencies are calling on the phone and banging on the door. Anger management, in contrast, is similar to using a budget to pay bills on time. Anger management opens up the "envelopes" of difficult situations and decides how to handle them responsibly. Disagreements are discussed as they arise, while they are still small and manageable. The way out of this vicious circle is learning assertiveness, learning how to bring up issues in a digestible way—not frightening, insulting, or threatening.

---

*Assignment:   Begin to determine which Vicious Circles are strongest with you.   Turn to Worksheet 5 in Appendix II, and choose the Vicious Circles that seem "right" for you, along with your reasons.  Then turn to the I-Rate Exam in Appendix I, and fill out the form.   Score the I-Rate using the score sheet.   Is there any correspondence between your guesses and the results of the I-Rate Exam?*

---

# INTERLUDE:
# Asking for Directions

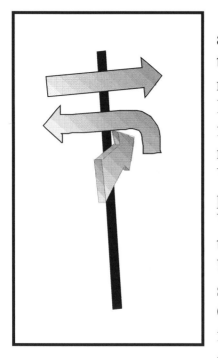

A manual is like a road, and we are at an intersection. Some readers, it's true, may have exited the road before now—it takes time, energy, and some level of honesty to have proceeded this far. Some may have read until now, but may not see themselves in any of the Vicious Circles, and may elect not to proceed. Others may recognize the Vicious Circles, but are satisfied with their lives as they are, enjoying the benefits they reap from the short-term surge of power that anger offers. Others may recognize the circles, but feel hopeless that anything might be done to break these self-destructive patterns. Others may believe they have ideas that will work to break these patterns without outside help.

Let's admit it—we as men are lousy at asking for directions, preferring to drive aimlessly at top speed across strange cities rather than rolling down the window and admitting we could use some help. Let's also admit that it's even somewhat embarrassing to be caught slowing down to peer at a road sign or to study a map. Only after all other resources have been exhausted do we stop and ask for help. The remainder of this manual consists of directions, road signs, or maps that may be used to break out of the self-destructive vicious circles we find ourselves in. It involves a program of self-study, because there is no single correct route out of the mess of our lives—each mess is different. It requires work—observation, decision, and effort—but it can be done.

*Exercise: Anger Balance Sheet. Turn to Worksheet 4 in Appendix II and fill out the Anger Balance Sheet. This will help you start to weigh anger as it is in your life now, comparing the benefits from the liabilities.*

# II. MAD SCIENCE

Let's imagine that the anger in our lives is an enemy, and it has ways of attacking our lives suddenly, causing major damage. If we were planning a battle, we would first need to research the enemy, find out everything we could about them—where their weapons are amassed, what their troop strength is, what their main battle tactics are. We might send spies behind enemy lines, or gather reconnaissance photos. It would be a mistake to mount our counter-attack before we had gathered the intelligence. Let's spend some time gathering information before we do anything else: we call this *mad science.*

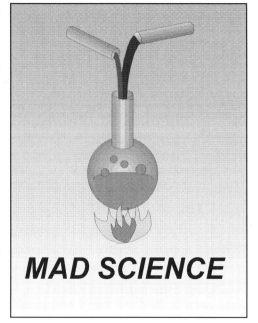

**MAD SCIENCE**

Mad Science is the science of what makes us mad. This means understanding the ingredients that go into an angry incident, the chemical reactions that take place between those ingredients, the melting point, how long it takes a reaction to occur, how toxic the reaction is. There is no easy way of doing this—a person needs to get into the laboratory and do what scientists do: observe, make hypotheses, and experiment with what works.

Our observations will not necessarily be sophisticated when we start. When people first observed the rising and setting of the sun, it seemed that the sun moved and the earth stayed still. It is only with generations of painstaking astronomy that the theories of the universe have shifted, and we realize that both sun and earth are in motion in a universe much more vast that the primitives ever imagined.

In the same way, we may find our theories about anger shifting. It is not unusual for a person to begin by thinking that his or her anger originates outside himself, in events of the world. "He made me mad" or "she pressed my buttons." But let's not worry yet about how sophisticated our observations are for now. Let's get started.

## Rage-Robot

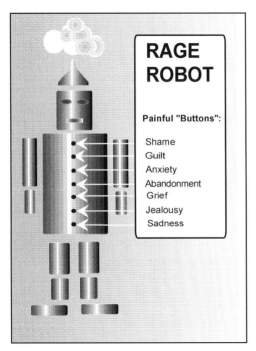

**RAGE ROBOT**

Painful "Buttons":

Shame
Guilt
Anxiety
Abandonment
Grief
Jealousy
Sadness

There is a common metaphor for anger which portrays the angry person as a robot—"He pushed my buttons." "I was only reacting to what he said." The "buttons" which are pushed are feelings of discomfort—shame, guilt, anxiety, etc. In this view, anger seems hard-wired, automatic, an unavoidable response to certain types of life experiences, where "Anyone would have gotten mad."

There is a classic genre of science fiction movie that tells of a battle between humans and robots—*Blade Runner*, the *Terminator* series, *Robocop*. The movie usually takes place in the distant future, and the humans and robots often look a lot alike, except for one or two distinguishing characteristics—a mark on the face, a subtle difference in speech, a whirring or clicking sound. Of course, knowing the difference is crucial. But in some of the films, even the hero turns out to be a robot.

I suggest that the real battle between robots and humans happens not in some future world, but within ourselves, between different ways we look at our rage. We often experience our anger as if we were Rage-Robots—as if our anger were automatic, triggered by events of the external world. The other view towards anger is that we are human beings, with free will, and that anger is a choice.

How can we tell whether we are humans or robots? The key distinguishing characteristic is the language we use. When we say, "She made me mad," "He pressed my buttons," "That was the last straw," we are saying that our anger was triggered by what someone else did. In this view, there is no anger management that can be done from within. The only way of stopping a robot is if someone else shuts it off or destroys it. On the other hand, human language is the language of free will: "I got mad not because of what you did, but because I made some unfortunate choices. I can do better," "You didn't make me mad, I made myself mad."

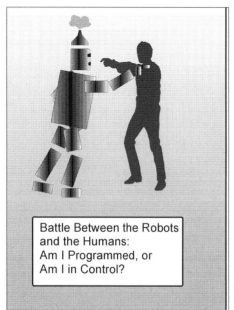

Battle Between the Robots and the Humans:
Am I Programmed, or
Am I in Control?

*Take a minute to look honestly at yourself. Are you one of the robots, or one of the humans? Are you a mixture of the two? Listen carefully to the language you use about anger, or ask someone who knows you well. This is a difficult question, and requires a sometimes-painful sincerity. If you can notice robot parts, that's a good sign.*

*In the table on Worksheet 3, write things you say about your anger in the appropriate column.*

# Anger and Freedom

According to research on the escalation of anger, when one experiences an insult—some sort of pain—a person's energy level rushes up, due to the secretion of enzymes from the adrenal gland, which may last for several minutes. During this time, a person is prepared for action—fight or flight, depending on the situation. Even after this energy rush dies down, a person does not return to the mental state he was in before the insult. Instead, he remains in a state of vigilance for some time. During this period, one is more susceptible to angry explosions. Small things can cause the anger level to rise quickly again. If a person has just gotten into a shouting

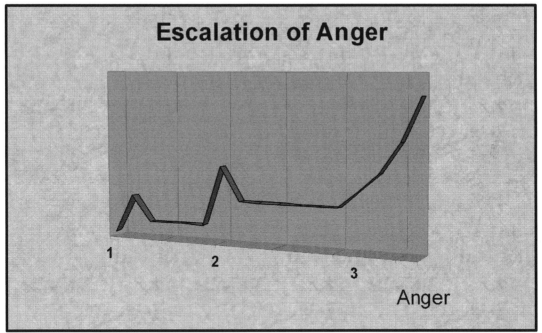

match with another driver, he may be susceptible to getting furious at his children kicking the back seat even after the other car has disappeared. Most of us realize that we get mad easier when we're already stressed. This is shown in the graph above, where anger spikes at insult #1, then declines, but to a higher level than before. At insult #2, it spikes higher, leaving the person even tenser.

The seat of emotion in the brain is the amygdala, a small, almond-shaped part of the brain that evolved millions of years ago. The amygdala has the job of recognizing danger and mobilizing the person to action—either fight or flight. This mobilization can happen even before we are aware of it. The neocortex is the outer portion of the brain, which has evolved much more recently. This is the area where rational thought takes place, and is the part of the brain that is responsible for conscious decisions. Every time something seems dangerous, there is an inner struggle between the slower, Freedom of the brain and the faster, more primitive emotional par... the amygdala runs things, the more automatic one's anger seems. The more the neocortex carries the day, the more anger seems a deliberate, thoughtful choice.

The metaphor of the Rage-Robot may give the impression that one is either an entirely free human or a robot which acts automatically. The relationship between anger and freedom is more complex than this. The graph below represents a hypothesis about an inverse relationship between anger and freedom. When one is calm, without a care in the world, he experiences significant freedom. With each insult, the level of anger rises, and the level of freedom falls. After passing the point on the graph called the Red Zone, one has high-level anger and low-level freedom. At the extreme of violence, one's sense of freedom is frequently quite low—one often reports that "I had no choice," or "He called me a jerk, so of course I had to hit him." One might even experience a blackout, during which one has no consciousness of choice at all.

Let's read the graph again, this time shifting from figure to ground. When one feels considerable freedom, he is not susceptible to high levels of anger. But when freedom is curtailed—during an argument when one feels the other person is cornering him verbally, during periods of unemployment when one can't seem to get ahead, or if one is part of a repressed social class—high levels of anger are

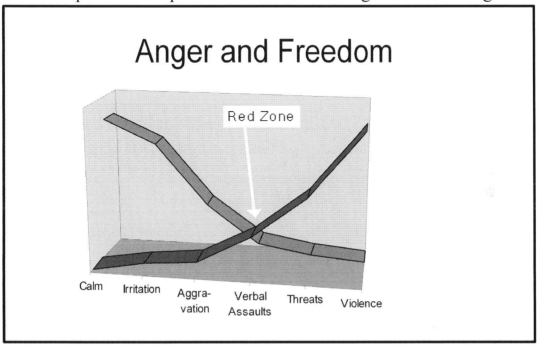

likely. When one has little freedom, he feels little power, *and the purpose of anger in these situations is to restore power--quickly*. But although the solution is quick, it is not lasting. When one has used anger to restore power, there is often a backlash from reality, where the power that was gained is just as quickly removed. A person might be arrested, fired, or kicked out of school. The key difference between robots and humans is this elusive thing called *freedom*. At the right part of the graph, we are all rage-robots, susceptible to angry explosions that seem sudden and automatic.

The time to use anger-management is when anger is low, because then we have more freedom. When a smoke-alarm alerts us of a small fire, we have many choices of how to put it out—we might smother it, step on it, pour water over it, hit it with an extinguisher. But when the fire becomes a conflagration, our options may be limited to stopping the spread of the fire to the next building. In order to manage anger, we need to develop self-knowledge—"smoke-alarms" which monitor our emotional states. But these emotional smoke-alarms are not available in K-Mart. They must be built through careful, dedicated workmanship.

## The Weight-Room

Lifting weights isn't easy—it causes bodily stress and strain, and it's boring. People lift weights mainly because it has results—muscles get built, a person gets physically stronger, healthier, maybe more physically attractive. Sometimes it's hard to get going by oneself, so a person might seek out a friend or trainer to make it more certain he'll follow through.

In the same way, it's difficult to break old habits in our relationship with our anger. The emotional strength we need to manage it gets flabby and weak due to lack of exercise. When we blame our anger on others, we never develop the emotional muscle necessary for managing it ourselves.

*A person develops emotional strength almost exactly as he develops physical strength: repetitive work against resistance.*

As in working on weights, developing emotional muscle is gradual, monotonous, and sometimes painful. It can also be rewarding--the beginning of a new, more mature life, with a sense of self-respect that can come only from living respectably. *You can do it.* But to develop emotional strength, you must push not against weights, but against something within yourself. What is this "something" we must work against? We might call it conditioning, habit, addiction to power, or vicious circles of behavior. But the name we give it doesn't matter to the work we do at the start. Let's not worry about theory now, not concern ourselves about what this "something" *is*. Let's look at how it *acts*, how it affects our lives.

# Anger Record

One key exercise in the "weight-room" of anger management is record keeping. Turn to the back of this workbook. You will see a number of sheets with the title Anger Record, with several columns.

| Date, Time of Day | Circumstance: Home, Work, School | Intensity (1-10) | Feelings (Other than Anger) | Thoughts | Actions | Grade A-F |
|---|---|---|---|---|---|---|
| Tues. 7/1 | Argument with Rebecca over gas bill | 4 | Shame, Helplessness | I've got to get this settled right away. She's being unreasonable | Yelled, slammed my fist, walked out | C- |
| Weds 7/2 | Driving: Guy tailgates me pulling out of work parking lot | 6 | Disrespected, anxious | The guy could have killed me. Get off my tail! He's a jerk. | Hit my brakes to slow him down. | C |
| Thurs. 7/3 | Son Lee yelled at his mom, called her a b**** | 7 | Disrespected, protective, worried | I've got to handle this right away. This kid is on the edge. | Yelled at him, sent him to his room | B- |
|  |  |  |  |  |  |  |

In the first column, make a note of when the incident happened. In the second column, summarize the incident in a few words. In column 3, rate the intensity of your anger 1-10, with 10 the highest.

The fourth column is the trickiest. Here, we want feelings aside from anger, and we are often blind to these. These are the feelings of discomfort that light the fuse of anger, and this fire is so small in comparison with the big blowup of anger, we often can't recall it at all. Several suggestions:

- Don't write sentences ("I wanted to punch him," "Why is he saying these things?")—these are thoughts. A feeling is usually an adjective—happy, confused, sad, stressed out, etc.

- If you find yourself writing "ticked off," "frustrated," "aggravated," or "irritated," ponder some more—these are just words for low-level anger. We already know you were angry—you wouldn't be making an entry in the Anger Record if you weren't.

- Ask yourself, "What was the other person trying to make me feel?" If you feel that she might have wanted to make you feel guilty or ashamed, this is an important key to what your fuse might have been.

- Avoid writing what the other person might have been feeling, and avoid judgments about them. For example, "I felt she was stupid" is a judgment about her, not a report about how you felt. You may have felt impatient about how she was acting, for example.

- If you find yourself writing fairly vague or general terms at the start, such as "disappointed" or "stressed" or "upset," don't worry. When Adam started naming the animals, he probably started with descriptors like "big," "brown," and "feathery." In time, your precision in identifying feelings should grow, with some work. In general, look for more exact words: what type of stress or upset or disappointment? Shameful? Guilty? Anxious? Betrayed?

In the fifth column, write down the thoughts you were having—the more the merrier. You may discover later the types of thoughts that were driving the anger, and you may also discover that certain thoughts were heating the anger up, and others were cooling it down. But for now, identify the angriest moment in the incident, and write down things that were going through your mind at the time. In column six, write down the actions, and in the last column give yourself a grade for how well you think you did, A-F.

How often should you make an entry in the Anger Record? Remember that this is the weight room, and to make progress you need to do repetitions. A person can't make progress developing his biceps by simply touring the weight-room or watching others do curls. Make an entry as often as you can—the more frequently and thoughtfully you make an entry, the faster you will see changes. According to research, the average person reports one incident of anger per day and seven incidents of irritation or aggravation. This totals eight possible entries per day for the average person—not a person with anger problems. Commit yourself to at least one entry per day. If you genuinely can't recall something that upset you for a given day, go back and mine old anger. Think of an angry event of a month, a year, five years ago and take it through the recording process. We can learn from old events, as well. No excuses. Don't let yourself off the hook—commit yourself to one workout per day.

---

*Assignment: Turn to Worksheet 6 in Appendix II, and spend some time filling it out, to anticipate potential obstacles in filling out the Anger Record, along with possible strategies that you might use to overcome those obstacles.*

# Driving Us Mad

As men, we are often quite comfortable driving a car, and when the family takes a trip we are often behind the wheel. But we are not as comfortable driving our emotional lives. We have too often left this job to women, and we have slid over into the passenger's seat. *The women in our lives—our wives, girl friends, mothers—know what we feel better than we do.* Ask your wife or mother—can she tell when you are anxious, upset, bored, depressed? It is time for us to start taking responsibility for our own emotional lives. We need to scoot over behind the wheel and begin to learn to read the gauges and make

the driving decisions.

Most men, when they drive a car, are very aware of the gauges on the dashboard. If the temperature needle is moving towards the danger zone, or if the oil pressure light is on, we notice right away. Obviously, the gauges are there for a reason: we want some warning that the car is developing problems before it is too late. We would never dream of taping over the gauges with masking tape before a trip, because then the first sign of trouble would be the smoke pouring out from beneath the hood. But this is precisely our strategy with feelings, the "gauges" of our emotional condition. Men typically tape the feelings over: they don't want to know how tense, sad, ashamed, anxious, or irritated they are. The first we know of trouble is when our emotional lives seize up or boil over, when we blow our tops. This is simply bad maintenance strategy.

The mention of feelings awakens shame in many men. We imagine wallowing like a wimp in self-pity, anxiety, or depression. It is not necessary to wallow in feelings to notice them, just as we would notice a dial on the dashboard. "Hmm, the shame-gauge is moving up," or "My sadness is diminishing." This does not require rolling on the floor—not that there is anything wrong with floor-rolling from time to time. This is simply important awareness.

> *Vocabulary of Feelings Assignment: On Worksheet 1, look at the various feelings listed, and place a check mark next to eight feelings that you feel you know well. Place an X next to eight that are foreign to you. Notice the distribution of the feelings in the different general categories. What do you conclude from the distribution of the feelings you checked or X'ed? What does this say about your usual patterns of feelings and blind spots?*

## Primary Colors

As men, we frequently have constricted emotional lives due to our blindness to feelings. A man I worked with in a group once remarked that the only feelings he knew were mad, bored, and hungry. This is an example of a common syndrome in men called *alexithymia*, which translates roughly as "not knowing the words for feelings." If we are only aware of boredom, rage, and hunger, this is similar to painting with a palette of only a few colors, missing the full spectrum.

**FOUR CARDINAL FEELINGS**

GLAD

SCARED    MAD

SAD

It is nearly axiomatic that there are four primary feelings, analogous to the primary colors of the spectrum: glad, sad, mad and scared. Obviously there are more feelings than these, just as there are more colors than yellow, cyan, and magenta. But these four are the basics. They are similar to the four cardinal points on the compass.

Glad and sad are obvious opposites, in that they represent opposite degrees of pleasure. Anger and anxiety are opposites, as well, but represent different kinds of movement in response to stress: fight and flight. When I am anxious or fear something, I move away, avoid, flee. When I am angry, I move *towards* the source of stress to change things. Anger is the change agent par excellence.

If I were well-balanced emotionally, when happy events occurred, I would be happy, when sad events happen, I would feel sadness, and so on. But we often find ourselves out of balance, so that one of the feelings predominates no matter what the life-event. If a person is unbalanced too much in the direction of fear, she may need treatment for anxiety. A person who feels sad disproportionately would suffer from depression.

Men often feel anger disproportionately. Anger then becomes the surfacing-point for all the other emotions. Instead of feeling sadness, a person feels anger. Instead of experiencing fear, he gets mad. Some people do not even realize they are in love until they experience jealousy—for jealousy may be defined as love transformed into anger. The picture above shows a spectrum of different feelings. If one

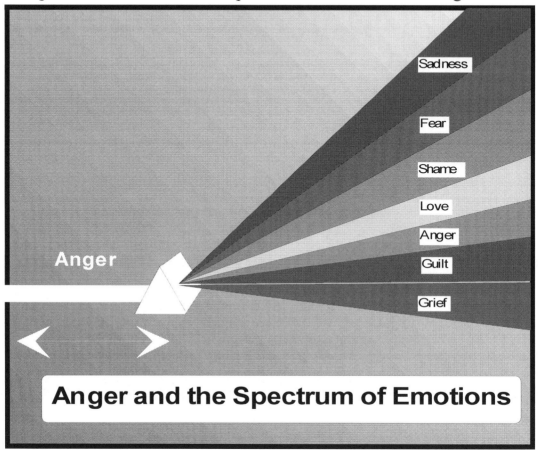

**Anger and the Spectrum of Emotions**

imagines the prism for a moment as a funnel, the full spectrum of feelings become transformed when they move through this funnel into anger, and the discrete colors of the emotional life are lost—mingled, constricted and muddled. To recover what we have lost, it is necessary to run anger through the prism to separate it into the original component feelings. This is one of the keys to anger management.

# Blowing Up

Anger is constructed like dynamite, with a fuse and an accelerant. A lit fuse is a small flame that will turn quickly into a huge flame (we call the huge flame an *explosion*) once the spark reaches the accelerant—nitroglycerin, in the case of dynamite. In the case of anger, the fuse is always a feeling of *discomfort*--anxiety, shame, guilt, sadness, or frustration. Sometimes this fuse is very short--so short we have no awareness of it. It seems then as if an event happens, and "I just get mad" right away.

The accelerants in anger are the thoughts rattling around in my head that transform the original feeling of discomfort into the angry explosion. We will return to these later--let's spend time now understanding the fuses.

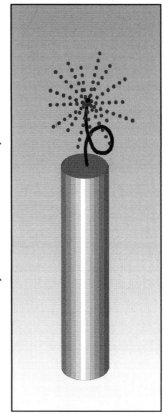

Anger is always a two-stage feeling, beginning with some feeling of discomfort. The discomfort is the fuse that sets off the TNT of anger. For example, someone steps on my foot. . . "Ow!" This is not yet anger. This is simple pain. It only becomes anger after I identify the source of my pain, then start to ruminate on why the person might have stepped on my foot and how I should respond. The fuse is some sort of suffering—physical or psychological. If it is psychological pain, it might be anxiety, jealousy, shame, disgust, guilt, grief, sadness, or disarray. Because of the way our emotional lives are wired, we are often unaware of the triggering feeling, and in our reports about the incident we may skip over this stage entirely: "He stepped on my foot and I got mad."

Essential to anger management is *fuse-lengthening*. Why? Because this allows the opportunity to ponder what we do. In the old westerns, when the fuse was lit to the dynamite or keg of gunpowder, the guys in white and black hats could punch each other, roll in the dirt, fall into the water trough, and shoot a couple of horses. Then, at the final possible second, the white-hat guy could pull the fuse out. *I want to be in this position: to have the opportunity to pull out the fuse.* But if the fuse in the cowboy movies had been an inch long, there would have been no opportunity for all the fuss, no chance to defuse the bomb. To make a decision, it is crucial that we have a longer fuse.

It is very important in anger work to *identify* the fuse of discomfort: what pain am I feeling that triggers my anger. Why? Because if I can identify it, it might be possible to learn to *endure that feeling of discomfort without making it immediately into anger.* If shame usually triggers my anger, then it might be possible for me to just feel shame just as shame. To do this, I must learn to lengthen my fuse. If I can lengthen the fuse a little, this increases the possibility that I might be able to decide whether, how, and when I express my anger.

Look at your entries in the Anger Record so far. Look at the feelings listed in the Feelings column, which—you will recall—are the feelings that came immediately before the anger. Do these feelings tend to be shame-humiliation, abandonment-jealousy, anxiety-chaos, frustration-claustrophobia, or upset-attacked? Get some initial sense for the main triggers to your anger. If I can learn to endure these feelings without making them into anger, this gives me considerable power over my anger. *The more I endure my pain, the more I can control my anger.*

# Surfing the Waves of Discomfort

When pain begins to rise, it is easy to assume that it will rise continuously until something stops it—until the source of the pain is removed. This is commonly where anger fits in: as an attempt to control and remove pain. For example, if I am in a discussion with

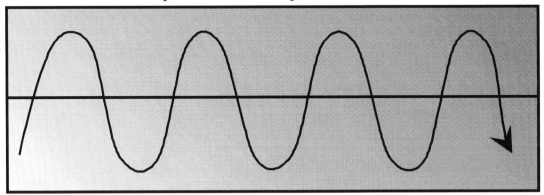

my wife over who should be responsible for paying a bill, this might cause me to feel shame, because I feel I should be more in control of our finances. Shame is quite uncomfortable, and I might well feel I need to act quickly, or the discomfort will go through the ceiling. Since I identify her criticism as the source of the shame, I could get suddenly furious with her in an attempt to stop the discomfort immediately.

Those who have studied pain closely, however, have noted that it does not rise indefinitely. It is structured like a wave, with crests and valleys. The hypnotist Milton Erickson suffered from two bouts of polio, and contended with his own chronic pain throughout his life. He observed that this pain was not constant, however. It might be very intense for a time, but if he became engrossed in a film or an interesting conversation, the pain would diminish and sometimes disappear. When my daughter was born, I attended Lamaze childbirth classes. When the pain of a contraction starts, it is the mother's natural tendency to tense up, to prepare for battle against it. But this is counter-productive, and can cause damage to both mother and newborn. Lamaze training attempts to help women relax in the midst of the pain, to let it roll over them like a wave that rushes in, then goes out again.

If we can turn ourselves into observers of our pain, and not just reactors to it, we will no doubt discover something similar. When shame, guilt, or anxiety begins to rise, if I watch it and simply endure it, the pain will rise, level out by itself, then decrease *even if I do nothing*. This is an attitude towards suffering that is much more common in the East, and is found in Buddhism, Hinduism, and the *Tao te Ching* of China. In the West, heroes slay dragons; in the East, they are more likely to endure them. If I turn myself into a hero of endurance, sitting and watching the tides of my emotions as they roll boiling in, then recede without my effort, my susceptibility to anger will diminish remarkably.

# Holding On, Letting Go

We all know how to become action heroes—we develop our physical strength, our self-reliance, our courage. Most male initiation rituals in our society—the military, sports, street gangs, Outward Bound—are aimed at making us better action heroes. We have many opportunities to practice muscular tension, which develops the strength to act with power. We have infomercials pitching exercise equipment that will help us have abs and pecs like Schwarzenegger and Stallone, and Tony Robbins (himself with abs and pecs like Schwarzenegger) training executives and would-be executives in personal power. But how do we develop the skills of emotional endurance? We could turn to Buddhism or some other form of meditation for answers. But—unexpectedly—we may find an indication in one of our great cultural icons: King Kong.

King Kong loved Fay Wray, but when he grabbed her in the jungle and later in New York City, she felt only the power of his grip, and was terrified. Later, atop the Empire State Building, perhaps when he realized he was dying, he let her go. There were two gestures of loving for King Kong: holding on and letting go. King Kong no doubt felt that his holding on was a way of loving. But when a partner holds on, this does not feel like love--it feels like being overpowered and controlled by another. When the partner opens the palm, it feels more like love. Fay Wray didn't know King Kong loved her until he let her go. In our rage we treat women like property—*my* wife, *my* girl friend. Anger often is the muscle we use to try to hold our lives together, or hold others to us, like a clenched fist. This is why we must practice the open hand.

## Exercise:

*Find a place you can relax, sitting or lying down. Feel your arms and hands relaxed on the surface next to you. Close your eyes and think of something in your life you are holding on to—a relationship, bitterness over something someone has done to you, some old habit you can't let go of.*

*Now with the rest of your body relaxed, and still thinking or picturing the thing you are holding onto, make a fist, with either your left or right hand. Close the fist about as tightly as you are holding onto this part of your life, and just feel the tension of the holding on.*

*Now slowly tighten your fist. As you do, imagine you are holding onto this part of your life even more tightly. Feel the tension as it climbs up your arm and spreads to the rest of your body—your shoulder, neck, head, eyes, back. Now tighten up the fist even more, as if you don't want to let go, are not yet ready to let go.*

*Now we will do something with your fist that you may not be quite ready to do in your life. You no longer need to hold on with your fist, and you may relax it when you are ready, feeling the tension drain from your hand, arm, neck, head, eyes, back.*

*If your fist is still closed, imagine small threads gently tugging the fingers open. You may feel the tingling as the blood flows more freely through your hand again. You may also feel the openness of your hand, the softness of your palm as it meets the cool air.*

*Feel this openness as the relaxation spreads to your whole body as you simply feel the letting go. And after you have dwelt in this letting go, you may feel yourself gradually returning to awareness of the world around you, and you may feel your eyes wanting to open, wanting to return to wakefulness.*

# Inflammatory and Extinguishing Thoughts

| | Definition | Inflammatory Thought | Extinguishing Thought |
|---|---|---|---|
| **1.** Targeting | Attributing the source of my discomfort to something external | Her criticism is making me mad. | She says what she says. I can choose whether it affects me or not. |
| 2. Personifying | Acting as if an inanimate object is alive and doing frustrating things on purpose. | That stupid car broke down again, like it knew I had just gotten paid. | The car broke down, like all machines do eventually. |
| 3. Malevolent Intention | "Seeing" what we assume to be another person's motives. | She said that knowing it would upset me. | I'm not sure why she said that. Maybe she just made a mistake. |
| 4. Extremity | Using "never," "always," "impossible," "forever," and other extreme-words. | This is never going to end. | This is taking a really long time, but nothing lasts forever. |
| a. Blaming | Locating 100% of the responsibility on one person. | It's all her fault. | I'm responsible for my part of the problem, she's responsible for hers. |
| b. Catastrophizing | Making mountains out of molehills. | If he doesn't stop it, I'm going to lose my mind! | I've made it through difficult things before, so I'll cope with this, too. |
| c. Labeling | Seeing a person in terms of a single, narrow characteristic. | He's nothing but a lazy jerk. | I feel angry about his failure to follow through |
| 5. Should-ing | Speaking as though we have the inside track on what is right and wrong for everyone else. | She's my wife, she should do it. | Nothing is written in stone about what a person should do. We can negotiate. |
| 6. Avenging | Believing that we have the job of ensuring justice, making things right. | If you hit me once, I hit you twice | If I try to solve this when I'm angry, I'll only make things worse. |
| 7. Empowerment | Believing I have the power to change things in someone else | I'm going to make her sorry she challenged me. | I can't change her, I can only change myself. |

# III. Inflammatory and Extinguishing Thoughts

## A. Inflammatory Thoughts

Behind every angry moment is the belief that my suffering is caused entirely by another personal being with malicious intention towards me, and that personal being is acting unjustly and immorally. If I don't stop the undeserved actions of this adversary, something catastrophic will occur, so simply enduring the suffering is out of the question. In short, anger cannot emerge without the belief in an evil enemy. When I get angry, I am under the spell of the morality tale. In this type of story, there is a villain who is afflicting a victim, and a hero tracks the villain down and brings him to justice, rescuing the victim. Examples of this genre of story are the detective story, the western, medieval morality tales that revolve around a rescue from Satan, and war stories. The villain has no positive characteristics in this type of story—he is simply evil: a Nazi, an oppressive rancher in the western, a criminal mastermind in a detective story, or the devil.

This belief in an enemy is so fundamental to the existence of anger, I will often distort reality in order to sustain my anger. I will force reality into the form of the morality story, even if it does not fit easily. I will transform complex, many-faceted individuals into the simple forms of innocent victims, scheming villains, and heroes, even if the individuals in question do not naturally conform to these roles. For example, in order to sustain anger, I will blind myself to any positive characteristics in the villain. Or I will blind myself to my own responsibility in creating my suffering. Or I will grossly exaggerate the danger of the situation, making it into an emergency that calls for drastic action.

There are several sorts of thought that make anger much more likely to occur. These thoughts are each basic conditions for the creation of anger, and they comprise something like an ecosystem for anger. There are many elements in an ecosystem that make possible the survival of a horse, for example. There must be water, nitrogen for the soil, oxygen in the air, and edible plant species. If any of these factors were not present, the horse could not survive. Similarly, there are several conditions that play a significant role in the emergence of anger. Six core thoughts make up the ecosystem of anger. These six are the basic building blocks that transform experience into morality tale:

1. Targeting: My discomfort has an external source.

2. Personification: That external source is a personal being, as opposed to an impersonal force of nature.

3. Malevolent Intention: That external personal source which causes discomfort is a being with malevolent intentions towards me.

4. Extremity: During the angering process, reality seems built from extremes—all or nothing, good or bad, safe or dangerous—with no gray areas. For example, in the angering process, the external source of my suffering is entirely evil, without the slightest good in it. If I am aware of the positive characteristics of a person, it is more difficult to sustain anger.

5. Self-Righteousness: I know what is right, and I am right. Whereas it is basic to anger to believe that the other person is an enemy, full of malevolent intention, it is also basic to anger to believe that I am entirely innocent and good, and that I have been treated unjustly.

6. Empowerment: Anger can only emerge if I feel power of some kind—power to have some impact on the behavior of the source of my discomfort.

If any of these six core thoughts is absent or muted, it is difficult or impossible for us to sustain anger. I believe that four of the six thoughts are *necessary conditions* for the development of anger: 1) targeting, 2) personification, 3) self-righteousness, and 4) empowerment. This means that if any one of them is absent, I *cannot* build anger. In an ecosystem, if I have all the conditions necessary for life except oxygen, life will not occur. Similarly, the absence of any one of these core thoughts is enough to prevent the development of anger. For instance, if I don't imagine my suffering as caused by something external, I can suffer, but I cannot get angry. If I do not believe that I have power to fight back against the source of discomfort, I may feel terror or devastation, but not anger. If I do not believe I am right in a given situation, I experience guilt or sadness or fear, but not anger.

The remaining two types of thought—malevolent intention and extremity—are *contributing conditions* to the development of anger. This means that they add significantly to anger's growth, but anger can still survive in their absence. I might become angry, for example, at someone who accidentally stepped on my foot. My anger would be significantly greater if I imagined that this person stepped on my foot on purpose, but I might still experience anger if I believed that the act was unintentional. I might also become angry with a person even if I did not believe that he/she was *totally* malevolent—without the presence of extreme thinking. Again, my anger would be significantly greater if I convinced myself that the individual was *totally* evil, that she *never* took my needs into consideration, or that he was *always* rude. But without extreme thinking, anger is still possible.

Let's look more closely at the six core thoughts that cultivate anger.

# 1. Targeting

Anger always begins with some form of discomfort—sadness, shame, anxiety, or envy. However, these feelings are not sufficient by themselves to produce anger. The first necessary addition is a target: someone or something that I judge is the source of my discomfort. For example, if I am experiencing anxiety, but have no one I can identify as a cause for it, I am unable to experience anger. But if another driver suddenly cuts me off, I have a presumed cause for my anxiety, and I can then make this into anger at the other driver. My thought process is something like this. "I am feeling anxious, and I hate that. That driver just cut me off, and that caused my anxiety to go up. If I stop that driver from doing things like cutting me off, my anxiety will stop."

There are times when a person might say, "My anger was mainly towards myself." This is common in situations of guilt and shame. For example, when a person makes a dumb mistake, he might call himself names, smack himself in the head, give himself long lectures about being more careful, etc. Doesn't this instance mean that it is possible to get angry without an external target? I don't think so. I suggest that when I feel anger towards myself, I have divided myself into three parts—1) myself-as-victim, 2) myself-as-culprit, and 3) myself-as-righteous-avenger. In the angry moment, I am identifying with the righteous avenger, contemplating the misdeeds of myself-as-culprit to avenge what has happened to myself-as-victim. I am regarding myself as something other, so there is still a target involved.

A targeting thought presumes an external source of my suffering, and sets the stage for a battle against that source, with the ultimate aim of ending my suffering. It is a thought that makes possible a declaration of war, challenges the warrior in me to don armor and go to battle. However, suffering is not only due to something outside of me. The Buddhists claim that suffering is a basic part of all existence, and would continue even in the absence of some external source. If I fully grasp this—that my suffering is not fundamentally due to the actions of another person—then my susceptibility to anger would reduce dramatically. In that case, I would simply experience my suffering, owning it as a normal part of all experience.

## 2. Personifying

In a memorable episode the British TV series *Fawlty Towers*, John Cleese plays Mr. Fawlty, who becomes furious with his auto

**Personifying: Turning Objects into People**

for failing to start while he is dashing about on some desperate hotel errand. He jumps out, points menacingly at the car and shouts, "I've warned you!" then runs off screen and returns with a tree limb, then thrashes the obstinate car. This is funny precisely because we know that an Austin Mini can't have malicious intent, can't be disobedient, can't have planned a breakdown on Mr. Fawlty's busiest day, and can't feel the pain from the punishment he inflicts. Yet in spite of this knowledge, we routinely direct anger at objects.

I suggest that anger is not possible unless I personify. When angry, I assume that my suffering is the result not of impersonal forces of nature, but rather of an external agent or being. Sometimes, it is easy to find an agent who, I presume, is responsible for my pain. When the utility company shuts off my electricity, I can direct my anger towards the indifferent employee on the other end of the telephone line. But when there is no obvious being towards which I can direct my fury, I will assemble one in imagination, because without a personal source, there can be no anger. When I bump my head on the pipe in the basement and instinctively hit the pipe, I am behaving on the assumption that the pipe intentionally hit my head and caused me pain, and that it is capable of feeling pain when I hit it. An object is just an object, without feelings, intentions, or sense perceptions. It is impossible to get angry at an inanimate object, *unless I make it into a being capable of malevolent intention towards me, able to feel pain, and able to change its behavior in response to my anger.*

In the study of religions, the belief that inanimate objects have a soul is called *animism*. In traditional societies, for example, people may believe that the wind and trees are beings with intentions, emotions, and personalities. We generally regard ourselves as beyond these primitive beliefs: we know that rocks and mountains are objects and not persons. However, whenever we feel anger towards an object, we inevitably revert to animistic beliefs.

## 3. Malevolent Intention

If I imagine that another person has entirely positive intentions towards me, it is virtually impossible to get angry. That is obvious—it would make no sense to be angry towards someone who, I imagined, cares for me, loves me, and admires me. It is difficult to sustain anger if I imagine that another person has mixed intentions—that they are partly positive and partly negative towards me. That might cause me confusion, "cognitive dissonance." However, if I convince myself that a person's intentions are malicious towards me or towards a loved one, then I can easily sustain anger.

It is most easy to sustain anger with offenses that I judge to be intentional:

sins of commission. It is still possible to become angry at sins of omission—if I imagine that a person caused my suffering unintentionally: stepped on my toe by accident, or unwittingly paid too little of the restaurant bill. In these situations, the anger arises due to the person's lack of vigilance and care. The anger is significantly amplified if I imagine that the suffering was caused intentionally, however. Anger is a defensive emotion, and surfaces in order to go to war, to engage an enemy.

## 4. Extremity

When I experience suffering, and believe that my suffering is caused by an external being with malevolent intention towards me, I can exacerbate the anger by thinking in terms of extremes: always or never, all or nothing, *totally* your fault, *complete* jerk. When we think in an all-or-nothing way, there is no middle ground. A person either loves me or despises me, I either succeed or I fail, I'm either at the top of the mountain or lying miserably at the bottom. We have difficulty seeing ourselves or others in between, have eyes that cannot perceive the gray tones between the white and the black.

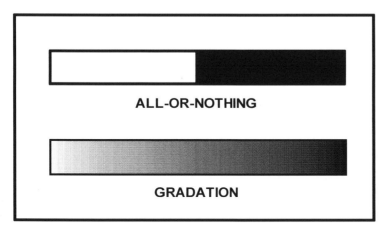

In reality, in most aspects of life, there are many degrees of difference between things. On a scale of one to ten, she might love me at level five. I may not have gotten a perfect grade on the exam, but I didn't get a zero, either. The world is a world of mixtures, gradations, betweenness, nuances, and degrees. If I see it in this way, I am much less prone to the sort of thinking that sees good and evil, black-hatted enemies, and hostile acts. If I think in terms of gradations, I can see a small amount of positive potential within every negative act or word.

As in the case of Malevolent Intention, it is still possible to sustain anger in the absence of extreme thinking. If I see things in terms of grays and gradations, however, the anger is generally moderate—proportionate to the situation, not exaggerated. Extreme thinking takes a number of different forms: a) Blaming, b) Catastrophizing, or exaggerating the dangerous consequences of an action, and c) Labeling.

## a. Blaming

A blaming thought attributes 100% of the fault to one person when there is some problem. It finds a single, simple cause for every experience of discomfort. Let's say I am walking down the aisle of a bus and trip over a man's foot, causing me to fall. I might quickly generate anger towards the man whose foot was in the aisle. However, if I examine this situation with some care, the causes of my falling are in fact multiple. While I was walking down the aisle, a friend waved at me from the back of the bus,

indicating that there was a vacant seat. If the friend had not waved just then, I might have noticed the foot in the aisle, and I wouldn't have tripped. So the friend is a partial cause of my fall. I could have easily taken a seat closer to the front of the bus, rather than walk back towards my friend. I could have also decided to watch the aisle more carefully as I made my way to the back. Therefore I am partly responsible for my fall. The bus driver had pulled away from the curb before I reached my seat, and the lurching movement of the bus made me more unsteady while I walked, so the bus driver bears partial responsibility for my fall. I was carrying a bag of groceries that my wife had asked me to purchase, and the bag partially obstructed my view of the floor of the bus. So my wife is a partial cause of my fall. The designers of the bus made the decision to squeeze two extra seats on the bus in order to allow for more passengers— an important economic factor when the bus company purchased the buses in their fleet. As a result of these decisions, it is often difficult for tall people to sit comfortably on the bus without putting a foot in the aisle. So the bus designers and the transit company that purchased the bus are partially responsible for my fall. My bank turned me down when I applied for an auto loan, and if I had been driving my new car, I would not have been riding the bus that day, and would not have fallen. So my bank, and the

Federal Reserve which establishes the interest rates that the banks pass onto customers, were the partial causes of my fall.

This judicious inquiry into the causes of my fall very quickly becomes a wide net, a net which may eventually include the founding fathers of America, the inventors of the internal combustion engine, and the personal deity (if there is one) who decided that the universe would be improved by the inclusion of the force of gravity. After my fall, I whirled around and directed my anger on that poor man with the foot in the aisle. If I imagine that I had whirled around and had instead seen the vast assembly of persons and forces, numbering in the thousands or millions, which had collaborated to cause my fall, I doubt whether I could have sustained anger at such an enormous crowd.

When I get angry, I attribute blame for my discomfort in a quick, crude way—oversimplifying the situation drastically. I only see those things or persons that are in the foreground, and the larger causal matrix remains entirely invisible to me.

## b. Catastrophizing

One core belief at the root of anger is the belief that something *matters*. If I believe that the offense, slight, or discomfort is insignificant, it is easy to let it pass. "No big deal-- it's a small thing." But if I 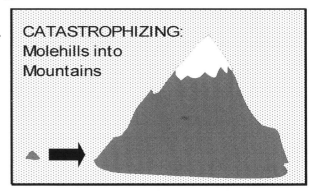 convince myself that the event is of great and lasting consequence, I can easily create anger. I can declare war on whomever I deem to be the source of the offense.

Chicken Little ran around the chicken coop, shouting to all who would listen that the sky was falling. She was *catastrophizing,* making molehills into mountains. This is a way of thinking big, and it excites anger because it makes our emergency signals light up, suggests that we need to respond *right now* to a situation because it is a disaster in the making. This style of thinking emerges from anxiety. By catastrophizing, a man can easily convince himself that his wife is planning to divorce him if she seems cold and unresponsive. One can convince himself that he must act quickly and decisively to correct a child's misbehaviors, because unless he acts promptly the child may become a drug abuser or a criminal. If a person catastrophizes frequently, it is important to practice observing things dispassionately as they are, and not make guesses about where these things might eventually lead.

## c. Labeling

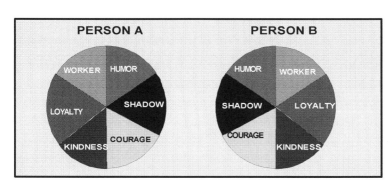

Labeling is a type of extreme thinking that involves seeing a person as a Nothing-But— sees the entire person in terms of a single characteristic. Each person is a mixture of many characteristics: a person is smart and stupid, funny, dangerous, ridiculous, sad, and respectable. All these things are true, to a degree. Usually, when a person acts negatively towards another, this negative can be placed in the context of the other, more positive characteristics the person possesses, and no severe damage is done to the relationship. If we were friends and you shouted at me, I might place this negative experience into the larger context of all the things I know about you. I could simply say to myself, "He's having a bad day," thinking of all the days that you were

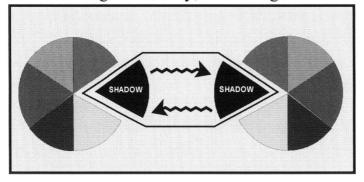

kind and tolerant towards me, and that would be the end.

When I start to label a person, I will take one negative characteristic—a person's honesty, for example—and convince myself that this is the only true thing about him. "He is a dishonest person." This casts him as a villain in a morality story, and gives me a license to treat him in a negative way. If someone is dishonest to me, for example, that entitles me to be dishonest in return, or to do something else to get revenge. This becomes a self-fulfilling prophecy. When I label someone negatively, then act negatively towards him, he is likely to start judging me negatively in return. The following is an example of a sequence of events that represents a downward spiral in the relationship:

- My neighbor John borrowed my lawnmower and returned it broken, saying nothing about it to me.
- I privately label John as dishonest.
- I start to treat John differently, because I have a "dishonesty license." I'm cold to him, and don't return the air compressor I borrowed.
- John notices my changed behavior, and notices that I haven't returned his air compressor.
- John privately labels me as an asshole
- John now has an "asshole license," which allows him to treat me as one may treat assholes. He talks negatively about me behind my back, and suggests to the neighbors

that I stole a video game from his house that has been missing ever since a party last summer

- I hear from another neighbor that John is accusing me of stealing the video game.
- I add other negative labels to John, privately adding the labels "coward" and "liar" to the previous label of "dishonest."

When two people get caught in a downward spiral of this kind, I call this a shadow-dominated relationship. This type of downward spiral occurs in any kind of enemy-formation: divorces, wars, or the break-up of business partnerships. Changing a shadow-dominated relationship is very difficult. It always involves breaking

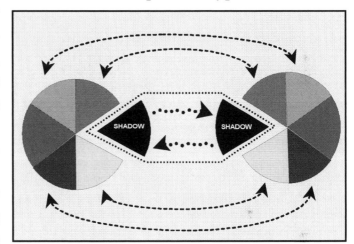

down the labeling process by recalling the positive aspects of the other person, reminding oneself that the other person is loyal to his friends, loves her family, or is kind to animals—whatever we can recall that might be positive. Gradually the rigid walls surrounding the shadow-dominated relationship can be dissolved, and the warfare can calm down.

# 5. Self-Righteousness

## a. Shoulds

There is no angry event that is untouched by a sense of self-righteousness. At the time of the anger, a person believes God (or some other supreme power) endows him or her with the duties of a prophet to judge the world and decide what is right and wrong. He is Moses, carrying the tablets, castigating the children of Israel. Even a man who goes to work with his guns and kills several fellow employees believes at the moment of anger that he is justified. It may be that after the fact, when he reflects on his actions, he may reconsider the virtue of his act: "Perhaps I was too harsh." Shoulds are invariably a dangerous addition to the chemistry of anger.

**SHOULDS: Privileged Views on the Workings of the World**

Does this mean that one needs to give up all his values? Of course not. Even if this were desirable, it would not be possible. Every instant of our lives we make choices: Should I go to work this morning? Should I eat a low-fat lunch or binge on burgers and fries? Should I watch a sitcom or the game? We are valuing creatures, and values are an ever-present aspect of every waking moment. But it is helpful to re-state these values not in the high moral language of descending from the mountaintop, but in the language of *preferences*. Rather than thinking, "No woman should ever yell at her husband" or some such pronouncement, it is less anger-provoking to think, "I would *prefer* she not shout at me." This allows one to hold onto values without tacitly assuming that these ideas are right and should be followed by all.

## b. Avenging

AVENGING ANGEL

*Don't Mess*

At its best, anger is a search for justice, righting what is wrong. One primitive idea of justice is contained in the motto, "Don't get mad, get even." This contains the seeds of dangerous escalation, because it basically says that one should not express one's anger verbally, one should instead act it out in a search for justice. Anger places itself in the position of the avenging angel, defending my rights and the rights of those I love.

What is wrong with justice? Nothing, except this sort of thinking doesn't produce justice; it produces revenge and dangerous intensification of conflict. Imagine a situation where two people each have the idea that one needs to "get even" for every insult or injury. In that case, we would have a recipe for rapid escalation, World War III breaking out in our midst. This is playground morality that needs to be eliminated if we are to slow the escalation process in arguments.

## 6. Empowerment

If I don't believe that I have power, anger is impossible. The seat of anger in the brain is the amygdala, which is something like a primitive computer whose role it is to make a simple decision in regard to threat: do I kill it, or do I run away? Fight or flight? The amygdala is center of anger, but is also the center of anxiety. Anger and anxiety represent opposite ways of responding to threat. Anxiety represents a retreat from the threat, while anger impels us towards it, with the goal of stopping the threat. In the evolution of our species, the amygdala has had an essential role to play in survival. The lightening-fast judgment it makes involves sizing up the threat, assessing its power, assessing my own power relative to it, and assessing the possibilities for escape. Anger can only occur if I assess that I have some power to stop or change the threatening behavior.

When I am stopped by a state police officer, I am not very likely to show my anger, even though I may judge that the officer treated me unfairly in choosing me from all the drivers that were hurtling down the highway. I may also judge that his manner was rude, that he was picky and sarcastic. In spite of these judgments, I am likely to be on my best behavior, to hand him my license and registration and follow instructions carefully. The reason for this submissive behavior is my quick judgment that I am less powerful than he is.

I am most likely to show anger in situations where I judge I have the greatest power. At work, I may be quiet, cooperative, and obedient to policies I may believe are unreasonable and demeaning. I may show anger only rarely in that part of my life, because the consequence of anger may be the loss of my job. At home, however, where I judge that I am more powerful relative to family members, I am much more likely to show anger. I may erupt towards my dog in a way I would never do towards a co-worker, because I judge that I my power is greater than my dog's.

Anger is a heroic emotion. When angry, I anoint myself as hero, battling the enemy who threatens a loved one or me. During anger I use whatever power I can to stop the threat, to achieve justice and righteousness. I am Achilles at Troy in the heat of the battle, possessing a divine energy that makes me invulnerable to pain and fear. It is common in traditional societies for warriors to believe that they assume divine power during battle. The word *berserk* comes from the same etymological root as the word *bear*. During the late Roman period in Europe, there was a class of German warriors called Berserkers, who were highly prized in warfare because of their unique ferocity. They believed that during battle, they were taken over by the divine power of the bear, and were able to fight with a bear-like fury, which made them invulnerable to enemy weapons. During any angry incident, I am possessed by a similar aura of heroic power.

At the core of the Empowerment thought is the presumption that the main route to power is through anger. During anger, I believe that the maintenance of my power is dependent on my asserting myself over the threat. I believe that I must undertake this battle to maintain dominance and control in my life. However, as we have seen during the discussion about vicious circles, the belief that anger produces power is largely a delusion. The power that anger brings is temporary at best. The route to true power is a much more gradual building process, not the adrenaline-bathed tidal wave of energy that anger produces.

## B. Extinguishing Thoughts

An extinguishing thought is a thought that calms. These are quite common—we use these spontaneously every day. We see these on bumper stickers—"One day at a time," "Shit happens," "Easy Does it" are all extinguishing thoughts. (Given An extinguishing thought is a thought that calms. These are quite common—we use these spontaneously every day. We see these on bumper stickers—"One day at a time," "Shit happens," "Easy Does it" are all extinguishing thoughts. If you look over the Thoughts column in your anger record, you may find examples of these thoughts which you are already using. For example, when another person is talking about you behind your back, you might experience an inflammatory thought that says "This is going to ruin my reputation." This is a catastrophizing thought which can increase anger. You may also notice yourself thinking, "Just

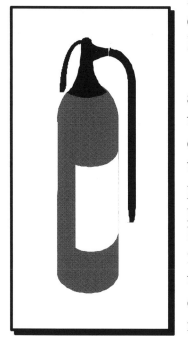

ignore them." This is a spontaneous extinguishing thought, helping the anger loosen its hold.

This is an important discovery—that you already have something that works like a thermostat, keeping your emotions in check. But it is not enough to simply leave this to chance. That would be like a primitive human noticing that rainstorms put out forest fires. At first, when a fire begins he might wish for a rainstorm, pray for rain, or even perform rain dances so that the storm would come and put the fire out. He might notice that sometimes the rain comes, and sometimes it doesn't.

Eventually, the person might decide to try master the technology of extinguishing fires by starting to carry water and use it to put the fire out himself, no longer leaving this to chance. Similarly, with anger we need to learn to master the technology of anger reduction, and this means constructing extinguishing thoughts.

In constructing extinguishing thoughts, keep these tips in mind:

1. **Keep it simple.** If we need a fire extinguisher, we want something we can begin to use quickly. We don't want to read several chapters of instructions (press Button A four times while simultaneously holding down Lever B, and it will scroll through a menu of options. . .). We want instructions we can implement quickly. In the same way, we need thoughts that are short and to the point.

2. **Keep it positive.** It is better to say to oneself "Think positive thoughts about others" than to say, "Don't dwell on thoughts like 'He is an impossible jerk who doesn't deserve to live on this planet because he makes absolutely no contribution to the quality of life here.'" Even though the two thoughts seem to have the same goal, the second one already starts us in the process of negative thinking and anger.

3. **Keep it relevant.** There are many different types of fire extinguishers, based on the type of fire one wishes to put out: extinguishers for chemical fires, wood fires, grease fires, etc. In the same way, there are many types of extinguishing thoughts, and they need to be designed for the particular type of inflammatory thought that is accelerating the anger. Look over the inflammatory thoughts in the anger record and think of extinguishing thoughts that would address these.

4. **Keep it handy.** Fire extinguishers are useless if we keep them in the carton and don't read the instructions until an emergency. We need to rehearse the use of these simple extinguishing thoughts in order to make them psychologically accessible. This can be done by first thinking the inflammatory thought, feeling how this increases anger, then shifting gears to the extinguishing thought, feeling how the anger disperses.

*Assignment*: Look over your anger record and notice the particular kinds of thought that recur. Create an extinguishing thought that might address that particular type of thought. You may choose one from the examples below, or create your own:

## Examples of Extinguishing Thoughts:

1. If I get angry, she wins.

2. I'm seeing his worst side, and he's seeing my worst.

3. Don't try to settle this when you're upset.

4. I don't know why she did that. Perhaps she was having a bad day.

5. Assume the best, and the best may come to be.

6. Happiness is the best revenge.

7. This is my chance to prove I can endure this with class.

8. If he treats me that way, he's not worth getting angry about.

9. Let's wait and settle this when we're calm.

10. Character is like a pearl. It's built from layers of patience.

11. Who said life is fair?

12. I can't change her, I can only change myself.

13. I earn respect by acting respectably, not by making people afraid.

14. Speak your mind slowly and firmly.

15. Will I care about this a month from now?

16. Take a deep breath and relax.

17. Let's try to settle this gradually, one step at a time.

---

***Exercise****: Rehearsing Extinguishing Thoughts. Sit in a comfortable place. Think of a situation where you got angry, and visualize who or what you were with. See it as clearly as you can. Hear the person's voice, and feel the anger rise within you. Feel the muscular tension in your back, neck, shoulders, arms, and eyes. Now begin to use the extinguishing thought you wish to try out, and while you are repeating the thought, notice the effect it has on your muscles in your back, neck, shoulders, and eyes. As you feel this thought calming you, assure yourself that this thought will be available for you in the future to cool things down and help you relax.*

# IV. Conflict-Reduction: Interactional Skills

## The War Against the Blob

It is easy to fall prey to the idea that anger originates somewhere within a person--in the amygdala of the brain, for instance. In reality, anger is a transactional phenomenon, happening in the space between people. It is a contagious, sticky stuff which descends unexpectedly on a relationship--a family, an intimate relationship, a work-team. If I am calm and you enter the room angry, I might quickly find myself getting angry, too.

The movie *The Blob* was made first in the early 1960s, then re-made during the 1980s. The story line in both is pretty much the same. A mysterious meteorite lands near a town, and an old man discovers a red, glutinous substance and touches it with a stick. It quickly crawls up the stick onto his hand, envelops him and grows. It finds its way into houses--under the door, through the ventilation shaft--and devours everyone within. The Blob travels towards town and engulfs every human in its path. The townspeople band together, study it, then finally manage to kill it with ice.

Anger is like this Blob: it is an alien substance--malevolent, infectious, and deeply disturbing. It can descend on a home in a number of ways: Mom or Dad can bring home stress from work, a son or daughter may bring in an attitude, and so on. However it enters, it spreads quickly, and before long it can swallow everyone in the family. It is quite difficult to kill, and teamwork and careful study are required to do this.

If we were part of a scientific team whose goal was to kill the Blob, we would study it first before beginning our attack. We would need to know its preferred food, its habits, its means of attack, its possible weaknesses. The Blob of conflict feeds on certain types of words and acts, and we need to observe this data carefully with the other team members.

# Exercise:  Blobbing the Family

*The following are questions to discuss together with family members, or with an intimate partner.*

## 1. How Does it Get In?

- *"Who brings the Blob in most often?  Second most often?" etc.  I find it helpful to break the answers down into percentages, such as the one below. Another way of rating this, especially if there are family members who have difficulty with percentages, is simply to give a numerical order 1-4 for each family member.*

|  | *Dad* | *Mom* | *Son* | *Daughter* |
|---|---|---|---|---|
| *Dad* | *10* | *20* | *50* | *20* |
| *Mom* | *25* | *20* | *30* | *25* |

| | | | | |
|---|---|---|---|---|
| **Son** | 80 | 3 | 3 | 14 |
| **Daughter** | 30 | 30 | 30 | 10 |

- *Fill in the names of your own family members in the chart below in a similar way, and ask each person to estimate the percentage of times (or cardinal order) each person brings the Blob into the household:*

| | | | | |
|---|---|---|---|---|
| 1_____ | | | | |
| 2._____ | | | | |
| 3._____ | | | | |
| 4._____ | | | | |

- *Draw conclusions from this: is there only one route in for the Blob, or several?  Is there any family member that everyone agrees is 100% immune from bringing in this sticky substance of conflict?*

## 2. How does it spread? *Questions to ask with the family or intimate partner:*

- *When the Blob does get in, does it spread slowly or quickly?*

- *When Dad brings the Blob in, who does it spread to first?  Who second?*

- *Do people feel the need to jump in the middle of the Blob right away, or do you hold back and decide on just the right time to jump in?*

- *Does it live in the house all the time, or does it take vacations?*

### 3. Effect of the Blob on the Family/ Relationship

- *Some families like arguing and fighting—it's like a game that the family or couple plays together like monopoly or something. What's the payoff? Is the family enjoying this or getting some reward? Is the Blob helping or hindering the family?*

- *If the Blob continues its work in the family without opposition, what will the family look like in three years?*

### 4. Blob-Enhancing Acts or Words: What Feeds the Blob?

- *I'm not suggesting anyone would do this on purpose, because I don't think they do. But if you decided one day you were going to try to make the Blob bigger—more destructive, more full of stress and arguing—what would you do or say? If you wanted to feed the Blob, what would you do?" Again, take turns, asking individuals first for a single example of a Blob-enhancing act.*

- *About other family members: If you were his or her consultant, and your job was to recommend something that would be guaranteed to make the Blob bigger and stronger, what would you recommend that she do?*

### 5. Blob-Reducing Acts or Words: What Diminishes the Blob?

- *Suggest one thing you could do or say that might diminish the size and strength of the Blob. Let each family member answer this question without suggestions from the rest of the family.*

- *Note: There may be several attempts at Blob-reduction going on right now, but sometimes actions or words which are* attempts to make the Blob smaller actually end up making it bigger. E. g., Dad saying, *"Just knock it off right now! Why do you always have to talk back like a jerk?"* may be aimed at Blob-reduction, but the result is Blob-enhancement.

- *Would the family notice if all of you did these Blob-reducing acts between now and next session? Which actions do you think would be noticed most? Which acts would contribute more quietly to Blob-reduction?*

- *If the family members each made a quiet commitment to slip in one of these Blob-reducing acts the next time the Blob made its ugly appearance, do you think it might have an effect on how big the Blob gets, or how fast it grows?*

## 6. Blob-Detector

- *It is often helpful for the family to keep a log-book of Blob-sightings, where any member can make an entry, with an estimate of its size, strength, and whom it swallowed or nearly swallowed.*

- *It is sometimes helpful for family members to take turns playing the role of on-the-spot reporter of Blob-sightings: for example, "This is Sherri, and I am speaking to you from the living room of the Manley household. The Blob has just made an appearance, and is now stuck to two... check that... three members of the Manley family. Details at 11:00."*

# Time-Out

Time-out is often emphasized as a key to anger management. One problem is that most people believe they know what a time-out is, and think they already use it. A person who stomps out of the room, takes a ride in his truck, has a few drinks, then returns as if nothing has happened is not taking a proper time-out. This person may be merely avoiding difficulties, and this can infuriate the partner, because she senses that her needs have not been heard or taken seriously. In sports, a game is won or lost only after *time-in* has been called, and the same is true of relationships. One must develop a track record for calling time-in, not just time-out.

A second danger is that one might misuse the break in the argument to infuriate oneself even further. A person might walk away, then stew and fume, thinking of things that would have been

better comebacks. One might use a concoction of such inflammatory thoughts as labeling, avenging and mind-reading to convince oneself that the other person really is a dangerous demon who needs punishment. If we Close Down, Obsess, Plot, and Stress Out, this spells out the word COPS, as in the illustration above, and this is a recipe for danger.

In sports, a time-out serves several important purposes. The four main purposes of time-outs in sports spell out the word COPE: 1) The coach *calms* down the team, when perhaps the game was getting away from them. 2) Time is taken to *observe* what has been happening—"Number 22 has been getting easy baskets because no one is covering him at the key." 3) A *plan* is made about how to deal with the problem: "We are going to go into a zone defense," or "We are going to double-team number 22." 4) The coach takes time to *encourage* the team: "Come one, we can do it, let's go!"

The same basic structure should prevail for time-outs in conflicts—Calming, Observing, Planning, and Encouraging. One should recall, however, that the opponent here is not the other person. The enemy is the *argument*, and ideally one should see oneself teaming up with the argue-mate against the argument. It is helpful to have a conversation with the argue-mate about this, which might start, "You know, I don't like fighting. This thing is tearing us apart. It's infecting how both of us feel about the other, and gets us to say things and do things we don't mean—for example, what I said earlier about your sister." For this team-building to proceed, it is crucial that one not sound as if one is blaming the other person for keeping the argument alive. It is helpful to confess what you have done to feed it and make it grow, and let the other person discover the ways they have contributed to it on their own.

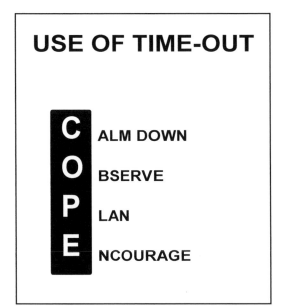

**USE OF TIME-OUT**

C ALM DOWN

O BSERVE

P LAN

E NCOURAGE

**Calming**. As I mentioned before, after an attack of anger, the human brain remains in a condition of high stress for some time, during which one is extremely sensitive to stimuli, often susceptible to misreading an innocent remark as an attack. *A break of at least 30* *minutes is necessary for the stress-level to diminish.* Distractions are often helpful—a quiet walk in a pleasant area, music, or an athletic work-out. I do not recommend a drive, because too often anger can become re-stimulated quickly on the highway.

When one leaves an argument during a time-out, it is important not to fume and fret over what one wished he would have said, how the other person had no right to treat him that way, etc. This is not calming—instead, the person is heating himself up, and when he encounters the partner again, he may be girding for war. The first step of time-out is to calm oneself: take deep, slow breaths, relax the muscles, let go of the issue. Keep going over the "Letting Go" exercise in this workbook to aid in this process.

**Observing**. Next, one needs to *observe* what was happening. This observation should be a calm, detached overseeing of the events that led up to the argument, watching as if from above. The anger-record is useful here: "I was feeling angry at a level five, and the feelings that were touched off were shame and a feeling of no-escape. The thoughts that were feeding the anger were..."

Not every type of recollection of the angry event is helpful, however. It is possible to recall the event in inflammatory ways, in ways that rouse the anger. I might think back on an event and say t myself, "I should have told him where to get off. He had no right to treat me that way. What I should have said is..." This obsessing on the should-haves and could-haves increases the likelihood of rage. In the proper use of time-out, the observation of the event should be detached, mindful, calm, and cooling.

Simply observing what transpired in a detached way is surprisingly powerful. It is as if one were moving from the stage into the front row of the audience, able to experience things with a cooler sense of detachment. "A watched pot never boils," and simply observing the anger changes it, adds a coolness which can prevent destructive boil-overs.

**Planning.** After calming down and observing in this detached way, the next stage of time-out is *planning*—not plotting. The plan should not be, "How can I beat this person?" but "How can I discuss this important issue with this person without losing ground to the argument--which is the enemy?" Planning for re-engagement involves setting a time and place that is quiet and without distractions. I often recommend sitting at a table, with each person supplied with a pad and pencil for note-taking. This formal arrangement can help people feel more safe, and can provide a way for one to make notes about what he or she wants to say while the other person is talking.

**Encouraging**. This step is often neglected, but it is crucial. My high school football coach rarely encouraged us, and we rarely won. We didn't have the faith that we could make sufficient changes to the way we played the game. There is not always a coach here to do the encouraging, so it is essential to learn to do it yourself. You are challenging yourself to do something differently, and this is very difficult. *But it can be done.*

If we were going back on the floor after a time-out in basketball, we would need to be prepared for *more conscious play*, keeping the coach's suggestions and strategy-changes in mind while we were on the floor, not drifting back immediately into the instinctive play which got us into trouble. Similarly, when we re-enter a conflict, it is necessary to do so with the eyes of consciousness wide open, because this is the only way we can break the old patterns, the vicious circles that have left us stuck. This is remarkably hard work. But if you have sincerely worked on the exercises in this manual, you are more prepared for the task. You have toned your emotional muscle, you have practiced the fundamentals of what you need to do to keep the eyes of awareness open. If you find yourself unable to do this differently, *go back and work on the fundamentals again.* No great progress was ever made in work, business, warfare, or relationships without this patient, gradual conditioning.

## Appendix I: I-RATE
### Individualized Reach Anger Type Evaluation

**For each of the following questions, rate your anger level, 1-5, with 5 being the angriest you ever get:**

☐ 1. if someone doesn't do his or her job.

☐ 2. if someone tries to control me.

☐ 3. if a person blames or criticizes me.

☐ 4. if someone won't drop an issue they know is upsetting to me.

☐ 5. when people overlook my needs.

☐ 6. if someone does something unfair to me.

☐ 7. if a person doesn't show me the respect I deserve.

☐ 8. if someone tries to tell me what to do.

☐ 9. if a machine breaks down unexpectedly.

☐ 10. if someone gets better treatment than me.

☐ 11. if someone I've trusted betrays me.

☐ 12. when a person makes a mountain out of a molehill.

☐ 13. if my partner (wife, girlfriend, boyfriend) is unfaithful to me.

☐ 14. if people don't leave me alone when I'm stressed.

☐ 15. if children I'm responsible for don't do what they're told.

☐ 16. if a person tries to force me to do what I don't want to do.

☐ 17. if the powers that be apply unequal standards to people.

☐ 18. if someone keeps bringing up things from the past that I've done.

☐ 19. if someone I love threatens to leave me.

☐ 20. when people laugh at me and belittle me.

☐ 21. when people think they can break the rules that apply to everyone.

☐ 22. if someone cuts me off on the highway.

☐ 23. when a person won't let me walk away to cool down.

☐ 24. when other people think they know better what's right for me.

☐ 25. if a person pushes me for an answer and won't just relax and wait for me to think it through.

☐ 26. if I've been punished for something and another person who did the same thing gets off free.

☐ 27. if a person I've loved thinks she/he can just close the door in my face.

☐ 28. when we've made an agreement and a person tries to ignore it.

☐ 29. when a person tries to rub it in my face when I've made a mistake.

☐ 30. when a person thinks that the rules don't apply to him.

## Scoring the I-Rate

In the chart below, add the scores for the questions, and enter the results. Highest total score is significant, but the highest score on individual questions should also be noticed. The I-Rate test is not a valid measure of intensity of anger, because it is based on subjective report. It cannot be used to compare the anger intensity of two or more persons.

| Avoiding Anger | Breaking Out | Mad About You | Rage For Order | Shame Game | Just Deserts |
|---|---|---|---|---|---|
| 4, 12, 14, 23, 25 | 2, 8, 16, 22, 24 | 5, 11, 13, 19, 27 | 1, 9, 15, 21, 28 | 3, 7, 18, 20, 29 | 6, 10, 17, 26, 30 |
| | | | | | |
| | | | | | |

# APPENDIX II: WORKSHEETS
# Worksheet 1: Vocabulary of Feelings

*On the list below, look at the various feelings listed, and place a check mark next to eight feelings you know well. Place an X next to eight that are foreign to you. Notice the distribution of the feelings in the different general categories. What do you conclude from the distribution of feelings you have checked or X'd?*

| ◆HAPPY | ◆RESPONSIVE | ◆ANXIOUS | ◆ASHAMED |
|--------|-------------|----------|----------|
| ❑ Comfortable | ❑ Excited | ❑ Frightened | ❑ Uncomfortable |
| ❑ Wonderful | ❑ Interested | ❑ Abandoned | ❑ Embarrassed |
| ❑ Special | ❑ Loving | ❑ Panicky | ❑ Humiliated |
| ❑ Loved | ❑ Surprised | ❑ Worried | ❑ Frustrated |
| ❑ Relaxed | ❑ Curious | ❑ Confused | ❑ Mortified |
| ❑ Carefree | ❑ Playful | ❑ Shy | ❑ Injured |
| ❑ Mellow | ❑ Funny | ❑ Distressed | ❑ Self-Conscious |
| ❑ Calm | ❑ Attracted | ❑ Alarmed | ❑ Disgraced |

| ◆DEPRESSED | ◆GUILTY | ◆ANGRY | ◆PROUD |
|------------|---------|--------|--------|
| ❑ Grieving | ❑ Terrible | ❑ Violent | ❑ Encouraged |
| ❑ Moody | ❑ Bad | ❑ Hateful | ❑ Good |
| ❑ Lonely | ❑ Awful | ❑ Upset | ❑ Daring |
| ❑ Discouraged | ❑ Contrite | ❑ Jealous | ❑ Important |
| ❑ Bored | ❑ Repentant | ❑ Furious | ❑ Strong |
| ❑ Tired | ❑ Sheepish | ❑ Mad | ❑ Brave |
| ❑ Sad | ❑ Sorrowful | ❑ Enraged | ❑ Self-Satisfied |
| ❑ Hurt | ❑ Sorry | ❑ Vicious | ❑ Arrogant |

# Worksheet 2:
# Cultural Influences

|  | **Cultural Influence** | **Messages About Anger** |
|---|---|---|
| **Favorite Cartoon Character:** |  |  |
| **Movie or Book #1** |  |  |
| **Movie or Book #2** |  |  |
| **Movie or Book #3** |  |  |
| **Song #1** |  |  |
| **Song #2** |  |  |

# Worksheet 3: Robot or Human?

> *In the following chart, write down things you say about your anger in the appropriate column.*

| Robot Things I Say About Anger | Human Things I Say About Anger |
|---|---|
|  |  |
|  |  |
|  |  |
|  |  |
|  |  |
|  |  |
|  |  |

# Worksheet 4:

# ANGER BALANCE SHEET

ASSETS | LIABILITIES

# Worksheet 5:

*Vicious Circles Assignment*: Look over the descriptions of the vicious circles and choose the two that seem most characteristic of you. Write down a few reasons why these were your choices. Then turn to Appendix I and take the I-Rate questionnaire, then score it, and see if it confirms your choices.

| Choice (in order) | Vicious Circles | Reasons for Choice |
|---|---|---|
| 1 | | |
| 2 | | |
| 3 | | |

## Main Vicious Circle from I-Rate Test (Appendix I)

1. _____

2. _____

3. _____

# Worksheet 6:
# Anticipating Obstacles to Anger Record

*At the end of a week of keeping an anger record, one might find that one has not followed through as much as one would have liked. If you fall short of your goal in terms of numbers of entries, anticipate the kinds of things you might say in a week if asked to explain what happened, and write these reasons down in the first column. For example, you might say in a week that "I simply forgot to fill it out,," "I didn't have the time," "I didn't see the sense in writing them down, because I think I can remember them without doing so,"or "I'm not interested in making headway with this right now." In the second column, write down some trial strategies for overcoming the obstacle you wrote in the first column. For instance, "Write a sign to remind myself to fill it in and hang the sign on the wall." At the end of the week, check how accurate you were about the obstacles. Were there other obstacles that emerged? How successful were you at overcoming them? Give yourself a letter grade.*

| | Potential Obstacle: What I might say | Trial Strategy | Grade |
|---|---|---|---|
| 1 | | | |
| 2 | | | |
| 3 | | | |
| 4 | | | |

# Anger Record

| Date, Time of Day | Circumstance: Home, Work, School | Inten-sity (1-10) | Feelings (Other than Anger) | Thoughts | Actions | Grade A-F |
|---|---|---|---|---|---|---|
| | | | | | | |
| | | | | | | |
| | | | | | | |
| | | | | | | |
| | | | | | | |
| | | | | | | |
| | | | | | | |

# Anger Record

| Date, Time of Day | Circumstance: Home, Work, School | Intensity (1-10) | Feelings (Other than Anger) | Thoughts | Actions | Grade A-F |
|---|---|---|---|---|---|---|
|  |  |  |  |  |  |  |
|  |  |  |  |  |  |  |
|  |  |  |  |  |  |  |
|  |  |  |  |  |  |  |
|  |  |  |  |  |  |  |
|  |  |  |  |  |  |  |
|  |  |  |  |  |  |  |

## Anger Record

| Date, Time of Day | Circumstance: Home, Work, School | Intensity (1-10) | Feelings (Other than Anger) | Thoughts | Actions | Grade A-F |
|---|---|---|---|---|---|---|
| | | | | | | |
| | | | | | | |
| | | | | | | |
| | | | | | | |
| | | | | | | |
| | | | | | | |
| | | | | | | |

# Anger Record

| Date, Time of Day | Circumstance: Home, Work, School | Inten-sity (1-10) | Feelings (Other than Anger) | Thoughts | Actions | Grade A-F |
|---|---|---|---|---|---|---|
|  |  |  |  |  |  |  |
|  |  |  |  |  |  |  |
|  |  |  |  |  |  |  |
|  |  |  |  |  |  |  |
|  |  |  |  |  |  |  |
|  |  |  |  |  |  |  |
|  |  |  |  |  |  |  |

# Anger Record

| Date, Time of Day | Circumstance: Home, Work, School | Intensity (1-10) | Feelings (Other than Anger) | Thoughts | Actions | Grade A-F |
|---|---|---|---|---|---|---|
| | | | | | | |
| | | | | | | |
| | | | | | | |
| | | | | | | |
| | | | | | | |
| | | | | | | |
| | | | | | | |

# BIBLIOGRAPHY:
# ANGER MANAGEMENT FOR MEN

Babcock, J. C., and J. Waltz, N. S. Jacobson, and J. M. Gottman. "Power and Violence: The Relation between Communication Patterns, Power Discrepancies, and Domestic Violence." Journal of Consulting and Clinical Psychology, 61.1, 1993, pp. 40-50.

Beck, A. Love is Never Enough. New York: Harper and Row, 1988.

Burns, Feeling Good: The New Mood Therapy. New York: William and Morrow, 1980.

Catalano, R., and D. Dooley, R. W. Novaco, Georjeanna Wilson, R. Hough. "Using ECA Survey Data to Examine the Effect of Job Layoffs on Violent Behavior. Hospital and Community Psychiatry, 44.9, 1993, pp. 874-879.

Cordova, J. V., N. S. Jacobson, J. M. Gottman, R. Rushe, and G. Cox. "Negative Reciprocity and Communication in Couples with a Violent Husband." Journal of Abnormal Psychology, 102.4, 1993, pp. 559-564.

Dutton, Donald G., with Susan Golant. The Batterer: A Psychological Profile. New York: Basic Books, 1995.

Goleman, D. Emotional Intelligence. New York: Bantam, 1997.

Gottman, J. What Predicts Divorce: The Relationship between Marital Processes and Marital Outcomes. Hillsdale, NJ: Larence Erlbaum Associates, 1993.

Hamberger, L. K. and Hastings, J. E. "Personality Correlates of Men who Abuse their Partners: A Cross-Validation Study." Journal of Family Violence, 1.4, 1986.

Jacobson, N. and Gottman, J. When Men Batter Women: New Insights into Ending Abusive Relationships. NY: Simon & Schuster, 1998.

Lerner, Harriet Goldhor. The Dance of Anger: A Woman's Guide to Changing the Patterns of Intimate Relationships. New York: Harper and Row, 1985.

Lohr, J. M. and L. K. Hamberger, Dennis Bonge. "The Relationship of Factorially Validated Measures of Anger-Proneness and Irrational Beliefs." Motivation and Emotion, 12.2, 1988, pp. 171-183.

McKay, M., P. Rogers, and J. McKay. When Anger Hurts. Oakland, CA: New Harbinger, 1989.

McKay, M. P., andd K. Paleg, P. Fanning, and D. Landis. When Anger Hurts Your Kids. Oakland: New Harbinger, 1996.

Meichenbaum, Donald. Stress-Inoculation Training. Boston: Allyn and Bacon, 1985.

Miller, Jean Baker. "Colloquium: The Construction of Anger in Women and Men," Work in Progress, Stone Center for Developmental Services and Studies, 1983, pp. 1-12.

Novaco, Raymond. Anger Control: The Development and Evaluation of an Experimental Treatment. Lexington: Lexington Books, 1975.

Prochaska, Norcross, DiClemente. Changing for Good. NY: Avon, 1995

Retzinger, Suzanne M. Violent Emotions: Shame and Rage in Marital Quarrels. Newbury Park: Sage, 1991.

Stearns, Carol Z. and Peter N. <u>Anger: The Struggle for Emotional Control in America's History</u>. Chicago: University Press, 1986.

Strauss, M. <u>Beating the Devil Out of Them: Corporal Punishment in American Families</u>. San Francisco: Lexington Books, 1994.

Tavris, C. <u>Anger: The Misunderstood Emotion</u>. New York: Touchstone, 1989.

Whisman, M. A. and N. S. Jacobson. "Power, Marital Satisfaction, and Response to Marital Therapy." <u>Journal of Family Psychology</u>, 4.2, 1990, pp. 202-212.

# Simmerdown Online Program

We have developed an online companion course to this manual, elaborating on these techniques, and providing further information, exercises, and reading material. This innovative course consists of twelve sessions, with narrated presentations, multimedia instruction modules, flash videos, supplementary readings, and online worksheets. For more information on this program, go to www.simmerdownonline.com. For a free sample presentation that introduces the program, go to the Angermanagers site at http://www.angermanagers.com/Free-Online-Video.html.

Made in the USA
Charleston, SC
30 May 2014